DAVENPORT'S OHIO WILLS AND ESTATE PLANNING LEGAL FORMS

(2024 EDITION)

written by attorneys
Alex Russell and Robert Maxwell

**SEE BOOKS AND LEGAL FORMS AT
WWW.DAVENPORTPUBLISHING.COM**

COPYRIGHT © 2024 -- ALEX RUSSELL

CREATIVE COMMONS LICENSE. This work is also licensed under a Creative Commons Attribution-NonCommercial-NoDerivatives 4.0 International License.

GOVERNMENT WORKS. No claim is made to copyright or ownership of government materials.

SOME STANDARD FORMS. No copyright or ownership is claimed of "standard" forms or leading forms for the state which are provided in this book, but fair use and privilege to use is claimed. Makers of such forms (often a state agency or hospital) have agreed by word, act, and implication the forms may be used and copied if no profit is sought and no substantial changes made to them. Such makers if not a lawyer or law firm are barred from profit or advantage in practicing law by making forms then limiting use. Forms and other related materials are used here for educational purposes only. Authors strongly believe in a religious duty to help people and do charity.

PUBLICATION DATA
(informal, library may use different data)

Names: Russell, Alex, 1972- author; Maxwell, Robert, 1960- author

Title: Davenport's Ohio Wills And Estate Planning Legal Forms

Other Titles: Davenport's Wills

Description: Davenport Publishing 2024

Suggested Identifiers: 9798367795615, LCCN 2021909030, 9798748423373

Subjects: LCSH: Wills--United States;
Wills--United States--Forms;
Estate Planning--United States;
Legal Forms

Classification: LFF KF755 .C55 2022 (or as library chooses)
DDC 346.73 Rus--dc23 (or as library chooses)

9 8 7 6 5 4 3 2 1 0 0 0 0 0 2 3

PERMISSION TO COPY AND USE BOOKS FOR FREE

To help people and groups the book's publisher and authors allow mostly free use by giving to all a "Creative Commons Attribution-NonCommercial-NoDerivatives 4.0 International License".

Basically as image below shows copying or use is OK if it still shows it's **by** the named authors, is **non-commercial** with no price charged, and has **no derivatives** which means no big changes.

Most users face no limit on copying, using, holding in a library to loan out, or giving out copies.

Permission is given to change margins and formatting, do small changes, and cut any blank pages that may occur (but double-check page numbers and table of contents page numbers).

Printing on only 1 side of pages avoids the problems with writing on back. Text margins are .75 inches. To do a book not a pamphlet increase left (inside) and decrease right (outside) margins.

Users can design a cover they like but the book title and author names must still appear on it.

Email questions to **davenportpress@gmail.com**.

(This work licensed under a Creative Commons Attribution-NonCommercial-NoDerivatives 4.0 International License.)

FOR FREE COPIES USE WWW.DAVENPORTPUBLISHING.COM OR BUY AT AMAZON.COM.

WARNING

THIS PUBLICATION IS NOT A SUBSTITUTE FOR LEGAL ADVICE. Publisher and authors say and warn this publication is not giving any legal, accounting, or other professional services or advice, which if wanted can be obtained by consulting in person an attorney or some other professional. **No attorney-client relationship or any relationship creating a duty or obligation is agreed to or created by the purchase or use of this publication or forms.**

**BOOKS AND FORMS FOR OTHER STATES ARE AVAILABLE,
SEE WWW.DAVENPORTPUBLISHING.COM FOR INFORMATION**

CHAPTER	TABLE OF CONTENTS	PAGE NUMBER
CHAPTER 1 - BOOK BASICS AND LIST OF FORMS		1
CHAPTER 2 - TERMS, PROPERTY, AND HELPFUL INFORMATION FORM		4
CHAPTER 3 - WILL BASICS		8
CHAPTER 4 - WILL GIFTS INCLUDING RESIDUE		11
CHAPTER 5 - DEBT, MARRIAGE, AND CHILD ISSUES		16
CHAPTER 6 - BASIC IDEAS ABOUT HEALTH CARE FORMS		19

WILL RELATED FORMS

CHAPTER 7 - FORM 1: WILL (STANDARD)		20
CHAPTER 8 - FORM 2: WILL (GUARDIANS)		24

HEALTH CARE FORMS

CHAPTER 9 - FORM 3: HEALTH CARE POWER OF ATTORNEY		28
CHAPTER 10 - FORM 4: LIVING WILL DECLARATION		34
CHAPTER 11 - FORM 5: DO NOT RESUSCITATE		38

GIVING POWER FORMS

CHAPTER 12 - FORM 6: STATUTORY FORM POWER OF ATTORNEY		41
CHAPTER 13 - FORM 7: GRANDPARENT POWER OF ATTORNEY		47
CHAPTER 14 - FORM 8: LIMITED POWER OF ATTORNEY OVER CHILD		52
CHAPTER 15 - FORM 9: DECLARATION FOR FUNERAL ARRANGEMENTS		55

APPENDIX: HOW TO GET FORMS AND SAMPLE FILLED OUT FORMS		58

CHAPTER 1
BOOK BASICS AND LIST OF FORMS

ESTATE PLANNING CONTROLS THINGS IF LATER ABSENT, SICK, OR DEAD

This book helps people in Ohio do legal documents to help control their health care, property, money, children, funeral, and more if later they are absent, sick, or dead. Doing documents to control things later like this is called "Estate Planning". People mostly have a right to control these matters so usually judges, doctors, and other people mostly ask: "Based on what a person wrote what did they likely want done?"

ESTATE PLANNING MOSTLY IS DOING SIMPLE THINGS IN 3 AREAS

Estate Planning is mostly doing simple things in 3 areas: Will Related, Health Care, and Giving Power. This book has 9 ready to use Ohio legal forms (but almost all people use just a few of these forms).

WILL RELATED FORMS

Form 1. Will (Standard) – this is often called a "Last Will And Testament" and this legal document lets a person control some things after their death especially who gets their property and money, who will handle doing things later as Executor, and if some costs and work can be avoided later by family and friends.

Form 2. Will (Guardians) – this is a Will with a part to name a Guardian of the Person to if needed (like if both parents die).care for a child under 18 and Guardian of the Estate to care for their property and money.

HEALTH CARE FORMS

Form 3. Health Care Power Of Attorney – this popular form lets a person just in case needed name someone as "Health Care Agent" to control health care and also if wanted write health care instructions.

Form 4. Living Will Declaration – this form does the serious act of saying stop most health care if later doctors determine a person's health is very bad, they are incapacitated, and more care likely won't help.

Form 5. Do-Not-Resuscitate – does the serious act of saying immediately from now on don't give C.P.R. to restart the heart or breathing, and this is a short form that is often used outside a hospital or similar place.

GIVING POWER FORMS

Form 6. Statutory Form Power Of Attorney – lets power over money, property, and more be shared during life with someone like a spouse, adult child, or good friend so they can do things to help.

Form 7. Grandparent Power Of Attorney – lets a parent share power over a minor child under age 18 with a grandparent so they can help control things involving the child including health care.

Form 8. Limited Power Of Attorney Over Child – lets a parent share power over a child under age 18 with someone so they can help control things involving the child including health care.

Form 9. Declaration For Funeral Arrangements – lets a person be named to control funeral and related issues, and this is mostly done if a person doesn't want closest family like a spouse or adult child doing this.

OHIO LAW ON ESTATE PLANNING COVERS MOST PEOPLE HERE

This book is only for Ohio since Estate Planning law and legal documents do vary a lot between states. <u>Usually a state's Estate Planning law applies if a person's primary residence is here</u> (often called "domicile"). Many judges say "residence" occurs if a person lives in a place and has no clear plans to leave. Later plans to move don't matter until people move. <u>People can stay under a previous state's Estate Planning laws and Will after they move</u> if people <u>always plan to leave the new state</u>. For example, people who move to a new state for months for travel, school, projects, or military often keep legal ties to their old state. <u>People often do health care forms for the state a health facility is in</u>. Most immigrants of any kind can do Estate Planning here.

ESTATE PLANNING OFTEN IS NOT VITAL AND WORTH SPENDING MUCH ON

Despite what many people think Estate Planning often does not greatly change the costs, taxes, delays, and work involved in these areas, so it often is not vital and worth spending a lot of money and energy on. Benefits seem very low for young people since only 4% of people die by age 50, and only about 0.13% of children before age 18 have both parents die. *See Social Security Tables by Felicitie Bell*; *Parent Mortality Census SIPP Paper #288.* Many people spend more time and money on getting some good life insurance.

BOOK IS SHORT, HAS FORMS TO QUICKLY SEE, AND USES EMPHASIS

This book is short and may read rough but can be read fast. Long books often lead to misunderstanding of the basics and skimming. This book has legal forms people can quickly see. For emphasis paragraph titles, underlining, and boxes are used. This book capitalizes some legal words like Will, Testator, and Agent but this is optional. To save space some small words are skipped and end quote marks put before punctuation.

THIS BOOK COVERS MAJOR LEGAL IDEAS AND SHOULD SUIT MOST PEOPLE

This book covers the big U.S. legal ideas on Estate Planning and major ways Ohio law is a bit different. This book can't cover all legal issues but should suit most people without some strange situations or wishes. <u>Strange situations or wishes that may need research or a lawyer include</u>: a) strange gift wishes for property and money, b) wealth over $5 million, c) big medical concerns like extreme age, d) property or money going to a person with a disability or special needs, and e) wish to move or hide assets to qualify for government help.

LEGAL FORMS CAN HELP MANY AND THIS BOOK HAS "STANDARD FORMS"

Legal forms are good at most things involved in Estate Planning and can make binding legal documents. Instead of legal forms a lawyer can be used for Estate Planning but this can be costly, take months of work, and they can make mistakes. In life people often pick a cheaper option. Importantly often a hospital, charity, state agency, or state legislature <u>has made a form most people use and call the "standard form"</u>, and doctors, judges, and other people may not like to follow anything else. This book <u>does</u> provide mostly standard forms.

LEGAL DOCUMENTS MAY NEED TO BE "WITNESSED" OR "NOTARIZED"

To be legally valid and enforceable some legal documents need to be "witnessed", which is someone watching the person doing the form sign and then the witness signs too. Some documents need to be "notarized" which means a person who is a "notary" sees it signed and then uses an ink stamp and signs too. Notaries (also called a "notary public") are at some banks, brokers, insurance agents, courts, law offices, libraries, and mailing-copying centers. Using a phonebook to find a notary willing to help is recommended.

The words "subscribe" and "execute" means a person signed a document, and "acknowledgment" means a person said a signature was theirs. If a person signs a document in a foreign language it is usually binding. When filling in a form it may help to know "respectively" in a form means "in the order just stated".

ANYONE CAN FILL IN MOST OF FORM, AND LATER TRY TO KEEP ORIGINAL

When filling out a legal form except for signatures other parts can be filled in by someone not doing the form with good typing or handwriting (pencil is allowed). Once done often people try to keep the original and hand out copies. Some people have everyone sign multiple copies to have many copies with ink signatures.

SOME LESS COMMON OR LESS USEFUL FORMS ARE NOT IN THIS BOOK

This book skips some possible but less common or less useful documents.

- A "Codicil" can modify a Will but it is easier and legally safer to just rewrite the whole Will.

- Some people do a "Pet Trust" to help a pet, but it's easier to just give money in Will to person given a pet.

- Some people do a "Revocable Living Trust" so a Trust entity with a Trustee holds property or money during their life, usually done to after death have faster transfer of things and avoid small delays, costs, or work of others (by "avoiding probate"). But this is rarely done as it may require moving most of a person's things to a Trust causing maybe years of hassle, mostly to avoid later small work for people happy to be getting things.

- "Childrens Trust" papers can be done (like as part of a Will) so at a death a Trust gets money or property for a minor child to manage until 18, but this is uncommon due to possible cost and hassle, since it rarely matters (as this book explains), and since most Wills already arrange other legal help for young children.

- Though separate forms exist usually organ donation in handled in drivers license or state ID paperwork.

- Unlike some states Ohio does not have a "self-proving affidavit" that is signed with a Will before a notary.

- Unlike some states Ohio does not let a short list or memo be used to later add small gifts to a Will.

PROBABLY DO NEW FORMS IF DIVORCE, MARRY, HAVE CHILD, OR MOVE

Divorcing, marrying, having a new child, or moving to a new state can have big legal effects, and if any of these events occur it is recommended people do a new Will and other Estate Planning papers soon. To help most states say a Will from another state is still valid if people move but this is not always certain.

NO FEDERAL, OHIO, OR OTHER TAX IS USUALLY OWED AT A DEATH

Usually no or little tax is owed as a result of a death, including estate, inheritance, or death taxes.

The Federal Estate And Gift Tax is the only Federal tax that may be owed due to a death, and it only starts when a tax credit is used up that covers $13.61 million a person in 2024 and later.

Ohio since 2012 no longer has an estate tax or inheritance tax that is owed at a person's death. For property or money in another state most states either have no applicable tax or, alternatively, have a tax credit that covers over $3,000,000 of things so owing such taxes at a death is rare.

A person's family or Executor may have to file <u>normal</u> income tax returns to cover the partial year a decedent lived and earned income in before they died. Life insurance payouts are usually tax free.

CHAPTER 2
TERMS, PROPERTY LAW, AND HELPFUL INFORMATION FORM

THERE ARE BASIC TERMS AND IDEAS IN ESTATE PLANNING

Some legal terms and ideas are basic to Estate Planning.

■ "Estate Planning" is about people doing legal documents to control things if later absent, sick, or dead. After a document is done people are mostly free to sell or transfer property, instruct doctors, or change forms.

■ A "person doing a legal document" and "doing a form" means the form is for and affects that person.

■ A "Will" or "will" (this book uses upper case "W") is a legal document done to control issues after death. The phrase "Last Will And Testament" is used since a "Testament" long ago was a small document done along with a Will to do some things.

■ If no valid Will is done a person is "intestate" and then a dead person's property and money is transferred to a spouse, children, and family as intestate law says. Some people a fine with this. This is covered later.

■ A person who died is called the "decedent" or "deceased". A person getting a Will gift is called "recipient", "beneficiary", or "heir" if related (they "inherit"). "Survive" or "surviving" is to be alive after someone died. The term "descendants" or "issue" usually means a person's children and grandchildren.

■ A person named in a Will to handle things after someone's death is called an "Executor", but if a judge has to pick someone they are called an "Administrator". The new ter m "Personal Representative" covers both these things and this new term is now commonly used in most Wills in Ohio.

■ A person doing a Will is called "Testator" or "Will maker". Before about 1995 a woman Testator was called a "Testatrix" and woman Executor called an "Executrix" but this is no longer often said or written.

■ "Probate" is a legal process to do things after someone's death like transfer property, handle creditors, and authorize a Guardian. Due to nice changes in law probate is now often informal, faster, and less costly.

■ "Property" is either: 1) "real property" which is land and buildings ("real estate"), 2) "personal property" which is things not real property, like cash, accounts, stocks, tools, clothes, cars, jewelry, and art, or
3) "fixtures" which are things tied to real property (like fences, posts, lighting, and wired-in appliances).

■ A person under 18 is usually called a "minor" and often a parent or guardian helps them do things. A minor or other person not reasonably able to make wise decisions lacks "capacity" and is "incapacitated".

■ A document giving power to someone is often called a "Power of Attorney" where the "Principal" gives power to someone called the "Agent" or "Attorney-in-Fact" (but they needn't be a real attorney or lawyer).

■ Ohio Wills are handled at local Probate Court. Ohio law is the "Ohio Revised Code" (often called the O.R.C. or R.C.), and each state law is called a "statute" or "section" (often shown by a "§" or "s" symbol). A form written into the law for people to find and use if wanted is called a "statutory form".

"ESTATE" MEANS PROPERTY OF DECEDENT AND ENTITY HOLDING THINGS

The "estate" or "probate estate" means all property and money of a dead person that at death or soon after didn't automatically legally go to new owners. Estate is also the name for a temporary entity run by an Executor to do things after a death (it's like a small corporation, e.g., "Estate of John Alan Smith").

PERSON CAN ONLY GIFT IN WILL WHAT THEY OWN AT DEATH

A person can only gift by Will things they own at death so people should research what they do own. Basically by law a person usually owns all they earn as wages and salary, owns their share of income and profit tied to property they own, and owns or partly owns any things their money buys or improves. And for property with "title" documents (real estate or vehicles) or where there is a "listed owner" (like accounts) the named persons are usually the legal owners unless evidence shows special circumstances. Note, a person during life can sell property, make gifts, or transfer things even if they are named in a Will, so people should consider if they already sold or gave away property they also name in a Will gift.

THINGS OWNED IN SPECIAL WAYS MAY LIMIT GIFTING IN WILL

A person should consider if they own real estate or other property in special ownership ways which may limit gifting by Will. Laws vary in different states but some common special ways of ownership are:

- "joint tenant with right of survivorship" or similar legal options, so then property transfers automatically to the other named owners regardless of a Will, which in some states is often how spouses hold their home;
- papers say a "life estate" exists, so then if life of someone ends the other people in papers get item; and
- "Trust property" occurs if paperwork made a Trust entity and then property was transferred into it or this is set to occur, so then the Trust papers control where things put in the Trust go after someone's death.

Plain "joint ownership" with many people owning a thing can occur if people do joint papers, all agree to it, buy with joint funds, or if a gift was to many. Wills can gift joint property, like "I give my half of boat to Ed Lu".

NON-PROBATE TRANSFERS THAT HAPPEN AUTOMATICALLY IGNORE A WILL

It is vital to be aware some money or property of a decedent may automatically transfers on death or soon after to new owners if certain arrangements were made earlier. This is called "non-probate property". Such things transfer as arranged even if a Will names the same items.

Examples are: a) a "designated beneficiary" form was done to name people to get an account or investment, b) transfer-on-death accounts were used, and c) real property is held by 2 people as "joint tenants with survivorship" or similar so at a death the surviving person gets things. Usually property in a Trust will ignore a Will and transfers as papers say to. Life insurance usually goes to the named beneficiary.

Trying to do non-probate transfers for all things is called "avoiding probate", but few people try this since it can cause years of hassle, benefits are small, and often some thing is missed. When doing a Will people should consider non-probate transfers that will occur automatically on death and consider what will be left.

"HELPFUL INFORMATION" FORM CAN TELL FAMILY AND FRIENDS THINGS

People can do an unofficial "Helpful Information" form banks, lawyers, and planners suggest so family or friends after a death will know things. People can staple records or lists to this. See form on next pages.

ESTATE PLANNING HELPFUL INFORMATION

For more space attach copies of form or blank pages. Keep pages by Will or other place for Executor or family.

1. Personal Information (Name, Birthdate, Social Security number, special family details, other):

2. Real estate, vehicles, and other major tangible property (especially if people may not find them):

3. Non-tangible assets like stocks, accounts, investments, loans owed you, and business interests:

4. Possible income or insurance like pensions, retirement, disability, insurance, or contracts:

5. Debts owed by you like credit card, loan, student loan, mortgage, car loans, and accounts payable:

6. Names and information of professionals used (attorneys, accountants, brokers, doctors, others):

7. Computer passwords and helpful files, document places, and safes or safe-deposit boxes code/key:

8. Other helpful things, wishes for funeral, special requests, and last messages to family and friends:

CHAPTER 3
WILL BASICS

WILL LETS A PERSON CONTROL THINGS AFTER THEIR DEATH

A Will is a legal document done by a person to control some things after their death. A person doing a Will is called the "Testator" or "Will maker". In Ohio a Testator <u>when signing</u> must be at least 18 years old, of sound mind (rational with sufficient memory), and not be under duress (unfair pressure or threat).

KEEP SIGNED WILL IN SAFE PLACE IT CAN BE FOUND AFTER A DEATH

A signed Will should be kept so it is found within days of a death, like in a desk, drawer, safe, with a person, or less often a safe deposit box. It may help to tell people how to get a Will. In Ohio before a death a Will can be filed in the local probate court for safekeeping but this is very rarely done. Ohio Revised Code 2107.07. If a person files a Will but then does a new one they usually withdraw the old version to avoid confusion.

A WILL IS SIGNED WITH 2 WITNESSES

WILL MUST SHOW IT'S A WILL AND BE SIGNED WITH 2 WITNESSES

Under Ohio law a document to be a Will usually <u>must show it's a Will by its words</u>, and the person doing it must <u>sign a Will in front of at least 2 persons</u> acting as witnesses who then sign too. A Will in Ohio just spoken including on a video or audio recording usually has no legal effect except in certain very rare cases. Ohio unlike many Western U.S. states does not let witnesses be skipped just because a Will is handwritten.

WITNESSES SHOULD AT LEAST AGE 18 AND NOT GETTING GIFTS IN THE WILL

A person to witness a Will must be at least age 18. It is better but not required that witnesses not be extremely old, not live far away, and not be named in the Will as Executor, Guardian, or to any similar job. Under Ohio law a Will is still valid if a witness is named to get Will gifts, <u>but such Will gifts to a witness later usually will be seen as void and won't be carried out</u>. Ohio Revised Code 2107.15. A small exception says a witness can still get up to the amount they would get if there were no Will under the Ohio intestate laws. To avoid these legal issues usually witnesses and their spouse are not named to get any things in a Will. Usually used as witnesses are friends, distant family, workers at a business, and strangers.

TESTATOR AND 2 WITNESSES SIGN THE WILL WHEN TOGETHER IN 1 ROOM

A person doing a Will should sign with at least 2 witnesses who also sign while all are 1 room watching the others. People showing others an I.D. isn't required but is common. A Testator needn't initial Will pages. A Testator or witness should <u>use their full legal name</u> unless they dislike and rarely use it. Witnesses only read the 1 paragraph they sign. Most Wills have people print their names and addresses. Testators legally need not say anything but often say a thing like, "My name is ____ and this is my Will which I do voluntarily and I want you 2 people to witness it". A person telling others it is their Will is called "publishing a Will". Some Testators chat a bit about the Will to help show they are of sound mind and know what they are doing.

OHIO HAS NO SELF-PROVING AFFIDAVIT SO MORE WITNESSES ARE COMMON

Many states use a "Self-Proving Affidavit" form that a Testator and witnesses sign in front of a notary, and this later helps "prove" a Will was signed properly. Ohio law doesn't allow this so after a death to use a Will evidence is needed from a) 2 witnesses to a Will signing, b) persons who know everyone's signatures, c) a handwriting expert, or d) persons with other evidence. Due to all this in Ohio to make things easier later some people and lawyers add more Will witnesses so 2 witnesses will be available later even if some witnesses die or move far away. In Ohio it is fairly common to have room for 4 witnesses in a Will, and people can modify a Will to do this by writing or copying in more witness signature and address lines, like:

_____   _____
Signature of Witness   Address of Witness

_____   _____
Signature of Witness   Address of Witness

_____   _____
Signature of Witness   Address of Witness

_____   _____
Signature of Witness   Address of Witness

USUALLY AT START OF WILL A PERSON NAMES ANY SPOUSE AND CHILDREN

Many Wills start with a place for a Testator to name current living spouse and living children. Natural or adopted child should be put here including any born outside marriage. People without this family can skip this or put "none". Not doing this may invalidate a Will by indicating a person lacks sufficient memory or mental ability, or may let a spouse or child not listed ask a judge to give them a share or all of the estate by saying a Testator forgot them. After listing family in a Will a Testator is often legally free to give them nothing.

MOST STATES AND WILLS SAY PEOPLE TO GET GIFTS MUST SURVIVE 5 DAYS

Helpful laws in most states and all this book's Will forms say if a person dies within 5 days (120 hours) or simultaneously with a Testator, then they are legally seen as dying before Testator. This skips the need to prove exact time of death (like if people die in 1 accident), and avoids a Will gift or right to something going to someone who then soon dies within days (so an item may have to go through multiple probate proceedings).

MOST WILLS SAY FAMILY MAY LATER DO "INFORMAL PROBATE"

Most Wills say after a death the family and friends may do "informal probate" which can avoid costs and delays. Informal probate often is done with just 1 court hearing and usually is done in well under 1 year.

MOST WILLS SAY TO SKIP COSTLY BOND FOR EXECUTOR AND OTHERS

Most Wills helpfully say no "bond" or "surety" is required for any Executor, Guardian, or similar person. A bond is insurance from a company to insure against misconduct. A Testator usually doesn't want a bond since the persons Testator names are trusted and them later needing a bond will cost the estate money.

MOST WILLS HAVE A "MISCELLANEOUS" PART WITH HELPFUL LANGUAGE

Most Wills have a "Miscellaneous" page with paragraphs of legal language to avoid some legal problems. This can help if later legal problems occur. A person doing a Will need not understand these paragraphs.

CANCELING OLD WILLS IS USUALLY NOT A PROBLEM

So a new Will is followed old Wills should be canceled ("revoked") but this is easy and rarely a problem. A new Will usually quickly says old Wills are revoked to cancel them, and all this book's Will forms say this. Or people can revoke an old Will by writing "void" or "cancelled" or "X" on it, preferably with a witness to this. Usually crossing out just part of a Will has no effect. Revoking a Will usually doesn't bring back an earlier Will.

A WILL NAMES AN EXECUTOR TO DO THINGS AFTER DEATH

WILL NAMES SOMEONE AS "EXECUTOR" TO DO THINGS AFTER A DEATH

Most Wills name someone as "Executor" to after a death do things like collect and give decedent's money and property to new owners, handle decedent's debts, and do probate. The law gives an Executor legal powers to do many things. If a Will fails to name an Executor a judge picks someone, but family may fight over who to suggest. The same 1 person can be named to be Executor, Guardian, and other positions. Note, many lawyers now use the term "Personal Representative" to refer to someone handling things after a death including a) an Executor named in a Will or b) someone named by a court called an "Administrator". Will gifts can go to an Executor.

EXECUTOR CAN BE PAID AND ESTATE PAYS EXECUTOR'S COSTS

Ohio law says an Executor can ask to be paid for their work, and a law says the pay is usually around 3% the value of personal property in the estate, 1% of the value of certain real estate in the estate, and certain other things. Ohio Revised Code 2113.35. Pay comes from estate funds. In reality usually an Executor skips asking for pay to not owe income tax on pay and leave more estate resources to carry out Will gifts. Expenses an Executor has like insurance, repairs, mortgages, utilities, funeral, attorneys, and probate costs are usually paid for with estate funds. Ohio law also says a lawyer helping after a death can ask to be paid "reasonable" compensation, and some counties have a suggested probate lawyer fee schedule which varies but is often around 3% of estate assets. But often the Executor bargains and signs a contract with a lawyer who agrees to a lower percentage, an hourly fee like $200 an hour, or a fixed total fee like $2000-$5000.

EXECUTOR IS PERSON AT LEAST AGE 18 BUT NEED NOT BE A RESIDENT

A person to be Executor must be age 18 or older and usually not have a bad criminal record like a felony. A person to be Executor may reside outside Ohio but being local can make later work easier and in some cases avoid some small fees and extra work. Ohio Revised Code 2109.21. Naming 2 people to both be Executor at the same time is allowed but rare due to the risk of arguments and delays, and since any 1 person named should be trusted. People can name a 2nd person to be Executor if the 1st person is not later available but most skip this since this rarely occurs and if needed a judge can pick someone. To add such a 2nd person a person could add: "or if they're reasonably unable to serve I name _____ to serve".

CHAPTER 4
WILL GIFTS INCLUDING RESIDUE CLAUSE

MAIN USE OF A WILL IS TO SAY GIFTS TO HAPPEN AFTER DEATH

Most people use a Will mainly to say what happens to their property and money after their death, usually by writing down various Will gifts to occur when they die. Verbal and even writings about this are not usually valid if not in a written Will. A Will can control property acquired after it was signed. The very end of this Chapter covers "intestate law" which says where a person's things go at death if no valid Will handles this.

GIFTING IN A WILL USING SIMPLE WORDS OFTEN IS BEST

Making gifts in a Will using simple words is often best, using words like "I give to" and "I gift to". This is legally fine and avoids confusing legal words like "bequest", "devise", and "legacy" which few people know.

A PERSON IS MOSTLY FREE TO GIFT THEIR THINGS AS WANTED

A person is mostly free to give at death their money and property as they want. But creditors a decedent owed money, a spouse, and minor children under 18 may have some rights which this book later covers.

IN WILL CAN DO "SPECIFIC GIFTS" TO GIFT PARTICULAR PROPERTY

Most Wills have "specific gifts" to gift <u>particular things</u>. Specific gifts can be any property, like "I give boat to Ed Blom" and "I give UBank account #84553873 to Sue Wu". If a gift is not clear the law assumes all of a kind of thing is given, like "I give jewelry to Ann Po" means <u>all</u> jewelry. But gifting specific property can have surprises like value of items can change, or a Will gift may later fail to occur if property is not owned at death.

IN WILL CAN DO "GENERAL GIFTS" LIKE OF MONEY

Wills can do "general gifts" where what is gifted is not particular property but can be flexibly chosen, like "I give 1 of my 3 cars to Ed Po" which lets an Executor pick which car. The usual general gift is money, like "I give $5 to Ed Hu". Money gifts are easy to write, let equal gifts be made, and are legally safer for many reasons. To carry out money gifts an Executor usually uses accounts or sells some property in the estate.

"RESIDUE CLAUSE" IS CATCH-ALL THAT HELPFULLY GIFTS ANYTHING LEFT

Most Wills by their end have a Residue Clause to gift property or money not already gifted in a Will or used other ways, often called a "catch-all" or "left-over" clause. This is covered later in this Chapter.

PERSON IN WILL GIFT USUALLY MUST SURVIVE OR GIFT DOES NOT OCCUR

Many Wills like this book's Will forms say a person named in a Will gift must survive (live past) the Testator for the gift to occur unless gift language specifically says different. If survival is not required for a Will gift what happens if a named recipient is dead can be unclear (state laws can be very complex). <u>People doing a Will should consider how Will gifts to people dying before Testator usually have no effect</u>. People if they see a person in a Will gift has died can re-do a Will or just let the Residue Clause handle it.

CONDITIONS ON WILL GIFTS ARE RARE DUE TO POSSIBLE PROBLEMS

Putting conditions on a gift, like "I give Ann Poe $90 if she graduates college", can cause problems like years of delay, risk of lawsuits, and big attorney's fees. Due to all this conditions are rarely put on Will gifts.

PEOPLE CAN ADD AN "ALTERNATE BENEFICIARY" LIKE FOR SPECIAL ITEMS

A person named in a Will gift dying before a Testator is rare, and if seen people can re-do a Will to name a new person or let a Will's Residue Clause handle it. Some people to prepare for this chance maybe for special items write an alternate beneficiary, like "I give boat to Ed Liu but if they don't survive me to Ann Liu".

PROPERTY OR MONEY IN A "JOINT GIFT" GOES TO MULTIPLE PEOPLE

The same property or money in a "joint gift" can go to many people to each get a part. For example, "I give boat and all hats to Ann Baxter and Mary Ann Swanson" means each person owns part of every item. People later can split things by agreement or an Executor can decide how to divide items. If a person in a joint gift has died their part usually is left to transfer under a Residue Clause.

CAN SAY IF PERSON IN GIFT DIES THEN IT GOES TO "LINEAL DESCENDANTS"

A Will gift can say it goes to a person but if they don't survive then to their "lineal descendants per stirpes". Descendants are a person's children and grandchildren. "Per stirpes" means "by branch" and is about how to spread property and money, and it mostly tries to divide things so each family branch gets an equal share. Most Wills use "lineal descendants" language in a Residue Clause. An example shows how it works:

A Will may say: **"Clothes to Sue Wu but if they don't survive to their lineal descendants per stirpes"**, and this means if Sue Wu has died and her son Ken Wu is living and her other son Ben Wu has died but left 2 children then, legally, under the law Ken Wu himself gets 50% and Ben Wu's 2 children each get 25%.

GIFT BENEFICIARIES CAN GET PERCENTAGE RATHER THAN EQUAL SHARE

If a Will gift goes to multiple people the law assumes equal shares, but if wanted percentages can be used to make unequal gifts, like "I give boat 90% to John Smith and 10% to Mary Baker".

GIFTS IN WILL CAN GO TO A GROUP OR CLASS OF PEOPLE

To save work a Will gift can go to a group or class of people like certain family if who is meant is later easy to determine. People can say roughly how much in total is gifted to be clearer. Examples are: "I give $10 to each person on my 2018 soccer team" and "I give $10 to each of my grandkids so this is about $100 in total."

LATER DIVORCE OR MURDER CANCELS WILL GIFTS

Ohio law says a person divorcing or murdering a Testator usually cancels all Will gifts to the person.

AFTER A DEATH FAMILIES OFTEN LET PEOPLE TAKE ITEMS UNOFFICIALLY

Ohio law unlike some states does not officially let a person use a short list or memo to add small gifts to their existing Will. But many families unofficially after a death let people take things of a decedent after their death in ways the dead person said, showed with stickers, or put on a note, and this is often fine. If people object to anything a judge often has the law be followed fully but later people can voluntarily retransfer items.

CAN LEAVE SOME WILL GIFT LINES BLANK OR WRITE THING LIKE "SKIPPED"

A person writing a Will can choose to not use some gifts lines in a Will legal form, like by just leaving them blank, writing things like "SKIPPED" or "NONE" in them, or using a computer to delete some gift lines. Judges and others usually do not care about neatness or empty spaces in Wills.

RESIDUE CLAUSE GIFTING ALL LEFT IS MAIN WAY USED TO GIFT THINGS

THE "RESIDUE CLAUSE" IS CATCH-ALL THAT HELPS GIFT ANYTHING LEFT

Most Wills by their end have a <u>Residue Clause to gift any property or money not gifted earlier in a Will or used in other ways</u>. Things transferred this way is called the "Residue". Many people <u>gift most their money and property this way by intentionally not mentioning in a Will most things so the Residue Clause handles it</u>. This avoids need to describe things and has less legal risk. After applying a Residue Clause if anything is somehow left then by law a decedent's closest heirs-at-law get things (this is their closest family).

USUAL RESIDUE CLAUSE HAS 2 PARTS

A short 2 part Residue Clause is usual and is used in this book's Will forms, and it has:

1) 1st space to name 1 or more persons to get things if they survive Testator (many name a spouse or closest family here), and if several people are named but only some survive then survivors split things, and

2) 2nd space to name persons to get things if all in the 1st space don't survive (many people name next close family or friends in this space), and if a person in 2nd space has died their descendants get their share.

<u>EXAMPLE OF 2 PART RESIDUE CLAUSE:</u>

"RESIDUE CLAUSE: I give money and property not gifted earlier, the residue:
   a) to   __John Paul Doe my husband__   who survive me with persons just named who survive me taking the share of non-survivors, then if anything remains
   b) to   __Sam Doe, Beth Wu, and Greta Fisher__   and if any of those just named do not survive me their part goes to their lineal descendants per stirpes."

In this example if John Paul Doe has survived he gets all things, but if John Paul Doe hasn't survived and also Sam Doe hasn't survived and he left 2 daughters then those 2 daughters split the 1/3 share of his (so get 1/6 each) and the other 2 persons in the second part Beth Wu and Greta Fisher get 1/3 each.

A FEW PEOPLE REWRITE RESIDUE CLAUSE TO HAVE 1 PART

A normal Residue Clause of 2 parts is often fine for most people. <u>But a few people modify a Will to have a 1 Part Residue Clause</u> since it tends to gift to a group more equally and be simpler to understand. People with no spouse and no young children are likelier to do this change, but even they often don't bother. See Example below for exact words to use if people want to change to a 1 Part Residue Clause.

<u>EXAMPLE OF 1 PART RESIDUE CLAUSE:</u>

"RESIDUE CLAUSE: The rest, residue, and remainder of my estate, and anything else I have an interest in, I give to   __Adam Doe and Beth Wu__   who survive me, and if any of those just named do not survive me their part goes to their lineal descendants per stirpes."

In this example if Adam hasn't survived but had 2 children they each get 25%, and if Beth Wu survived she gets 50%. Or if Beth Wu also hadn't survived and had 5 kids they split her part and each gets 10%.

MUST SUFFICIENTLY DESCRIBE NAMES AND PROPERTY IN A WILL

PUTTING NAMES OF PEOPLE OR GROUPS IN A WILL IS FAIRLY EASY

Putting names in Wills is fairly easy. <u>A judge or Executor assume a person in a Will meant people they know, so common names are OK unless 2 friends or family have the same name</u>. Details can help if names won't be recognized or to be friendly, like "I give $5 to my nurse Sue Ax" and "I give $5 to loyal pal Ed Lee". If people used a nickname "also known as" or "a/k/a" may help, like "I give $5 to Ed Wu a/k/a Big Fish". Gifts can go to a charity, government, or group, like "I give $5 to Shiners Hospital, "I give $8 to Columbus Metro Library, Ohio", and "I give $5 to Wix Church, Rex, TX". People often phone to get a charity's name.

PUTTING DESCRIPTIONS OF ITEMS IN WILL GIFTS IS FAIRLY EASY

Describing items in gifts is easy since people rarely own similar items. Often fine are gifts like: "I give ax to Ed Wu" and "I give big table to Ann Fox". It's OK to gift by category or list, like: "I give tools to Sam Lee" and "I give cow, van, and harp to Sue Hill". Financial assets can use plain words, like "bank accounts" or "stocks", but details can help, like: "US Bank account ending #1511". <u>Gifting using a location is riskier</u> as judges will ignore Will gifts if it seems items were placed to affect gifting and no "independently significant" life reason. So, "I give Ed Po items in safe and desk" a judge may not follow, but "I give Ed Po hats in attic" likely is OK.

DESCRIBING REAL PROPERTY IS HARD SO MANY USE RESIDUE OR TITLE

The easier and legally safer way to gift real property (real estate) at death is: 1) do nothing specific so it is handled by a Will Residue Clause, or 2) have a land broker or lawyer put names in a deed or a similar document so the named persons will get the real property at someone else's death.

Gifting real property other ways is harder though possible. Helpfully a Will gift of real property <u>described by location</u> legally does gift <u>all land, buildings, and fixtures located there</u> with no need to describe what's there.

It is possible to <u>gift real property at a particular address with very plain words</u>, like a house, fixtures, and land can be fully given by something like: "I give 82 Maxwell Street, Cincinnati, Ohio, to Mary Ann Brown".

People can do a <u>blanket gift</u> giving all of a kind of property, like, "I give all real property and fixtures in Adams County, Ohio to Ann Ivy Hill" or "I give all furniture and all bank accounts to Eric Paul Carlson".

Giving real property in a Will using a "legal description" is how many lawyers do it, but this can be hard to do. If using a legal description people must copy without mistakes <u>the full legal description of maybe many lines</u> into a Will with no abbreviation at all. A legal description might be found on a deed or on mortgage papers. Legal descriptions may refer to a "lot" or "blocks" on a map which is recorded in land records of a county, or it may refer to a path around the land borders with various angles, distances, and iron stakes.

SIMPLE WILL WITH MOST GIFTING DONE BY RESIDUE CLAUSE IS OFTEN BEST

Writing a simple Will without many gifts, much left blank, and mostly using a Residue Clause is often best.

If there is a spouse often a person does small gifts to friends and family, then uses the Residue Clause of the Will to gift all remaining to the spouse, and then names a few fallback persons in the Residue Clause.

If there is no spouse and no children often a person does a few small gifts, and then names some family or friends in the Residue Clause to get everything remaining.

A parent with young children if married to the other parent often does small gifts to friends and family, then in the Residue Clause gives mostly to a spouse, and then names children as fallbacks in the Residue Clause.

A parent with young children if not married or close to the other parent often does small gifts to friends and family, and then uses the Residue Clause to gift all remaining to the children.

INTESTATE LAW CONTROLS THINGS NOT COVERED BY A WILL
"INTESTATE LAW" CONTROLS THINGS NOT HANDLED BY A WILL OR SIMILAR

State "intestate law" which starts at Ohio Revised Code 2105.06 says if a person dies with no valid Will or also if anything is left after Will and transfers are done then certain surviving (living) family get decedent's money and property. Many people like intestate law and choose to skip a Will, but a Will often has benefits like avoiding costs. Note, "Descendants" means a person's children and grandchildren, and if someone has died who would get an intestate share often their descendants legally get that share.

Ohio intestate law says, in order:

1) if decedent (the person who died) left descendants but no surviving spouse, then the closest descendants get all (usually a person's children);

2) if decedent left a spouse and either no descendants or, alternatively, all descendants are related to the decedent and the spouse, then the spouse gets all;

3) if decedent left a spouse and either the decedent or spouse left some descendants not all of which are shared between the decedent and the spouse, then the spouse and descendants split things with some minor modifications that depend on exactly how people are related;

4) if decedent left any living parents but no spouse or descendants, then the parents get things;

5) If decedent left no spouse or descendants or parents, then the decedent's closest other surviving family get things starting with brothers and sisters, then cousins, and then other close family;

6) if none of the above persons survive then decedent's things go to the state of Ohio.

CHAPTER 5
DEBT, MARRIAGE, AND CHILD ISSUES

THIS CHAPTER COVERS CERTAIN ISSUES THAT SOME PEOPLE CAN SKIP
This Chapter covers debt, marriage, and child issues, <u>and some people can skip parts of this</u>.

DEBT ISSUES

PAYING DECEDENT'S DEBTS MAY USE UP RESOURCES AND REDUCE GIFTS
If a decedent had debts then creditors owed may ask a judge to be paid from decedent's money or property <u>before</u> Will gifts and certain transfers occur. How debts are paid is set by state law and a Will need not describe this. Funds to pay debts comes from decedent's money and property so may affect (in order) the Will Residue, Will general gifts, Will specific gifts, and non-probate transfers. Probate costs, health care, and funeral debts by law have some priority to be paid first. For certain reasons often not all debts are paid. <u>People should consider how paying debts may use up money or property, leaving less to carry out Will gifts</u>. A spouse and family usually aren't liable for decedent's debts unless they actually guaranteed or co-signed.

"FAMILY RIGHTS" MAY BE USED TO GET FAMILY THINGS BEFORE DEBTS
Most states have a few "Family Rights" a decedent's surviving spouse or young children can claim, and this may help let them get things even <u>before most debts of decedent are paid</u> and even <u>before Will gifts</u>. First, usually a surviving spouse or young children can use an "<u>Exempt Property</u>" right to get some of a decedent's clothing, furniture, tools, vehicles, and personal items for family to use to live. Second, a surviving spouse or children usually can use a "<u>Family Allowance</u>" right to get some of a decedent's money and property to live on a year. But <u>Ohio is unique and has 1 single "Allowance For Support"</u> that can be asked for, and this is split 1/2 or all to a surviving spouse and up to 1/2 to decedent's children under 18 not related to the spouse. Ohio Revised Code 2106.13. The Allowance is $40,000 in 2024 of a decedent's property and money plus up to 2 vehicles of decedent. Obviously if family use the Allowance this leaves less of decedent's money and property to do Will gifts or other transfers so may interfere with these. <u>So family don't bother to use Family Rights often a person gives mostly to a spouse or small children (like over 50% and family house)</u>. Some people may want to do research about this.

SECURED DEBTS LIKE MORTGAGE OR VEHICLE LIEN ARE NOT PAID OFF
Laws in most states say <u>do not pay off secured debts on property of a decedent</u> like a house mortgage or vehicle lien even if other debts are paid by Executor or in probate. This avoids using up estate resources on paying these usually big debts and leaves more estate resources to carry out Will gifts and other transfers. Due to this, all this book's Will forms say do not usually pay off any secured debts. But if a Testator wants they can 1) put in a Will an order to pay (like, "Executor pay off the house mortgage"), or 2) gift enough money to pay off a secured debt to the person getting the property. Most banks let new owners keep paying monthly a secured debt like a mortgage or lien on property that people got upon someone's death.

MARRIAGE ISSUES

OHIO LIKE MOST STATES HAS "SEPARATE PROPERTY LAW" FOR SPOUSES

Ohio like most states uses the "Separate Property Law" system that says a married person <u>mostly owns their money and property separately</u> and not jointly with a spouse. Due to this a married person is usually free to sell during life or gift by Will most of their money or property and not have to involve a spouse. But joint ownership by 2 spouses and not separate ownership <u>can arise in other ways</u>, like by agreement, both spouses paying part of the purchase price, if a gift was to both spouses, or if paperwork calls it joint.

"COMMUNITY PROPERTY" LAW APPLIES IN OTHER STATES FOR SPOUSES

There are 9 states that use "Community Property" law for spouses (Arizona, California, Louisiana, Idaho, Nevada, New Mexico, Texas, Washington, and Wisconsin). This says property or money is owned 50/50 by spouses as Community Property if it's from mental or physical work while married (like wages or salary) or if items are bought or improved with Community Property. People moving from these states may face issues.

"JOINT WILL" OR SIMILAR BOTH SPOUSES SIGN IS NOT RECOMMENDED

Some couples who worry try to do 1 "Joint Will" or "Contract To Make A Will" written by a lawyer which says spouses give all to the other if they die first, then says last living spouse gives to all children equally, and usually says a spouse may not change this. This is restrictive and banned in some states and is rare.

SPOUSE CAN GET "ELECTIVE SHARE" OF 1/2 OR 1/3 INSTEAD OF USING WILL

A spouse if unhappy with what a Will and other transfers may give them has <u>a right to instead choose (elect) an "Elective Share" of most of a dead spouse's property and money</u> rather than take what a Will says. To avoid this both spouses have to sign a pre-nuptial or a post-nuptial agreement written by a lawyer which can be costly. Most states have this law for a spouse for fairness, so a spouse has resources to live on, and so early divorce isn't the only way to be financially secure. Ohio law sets the Elective Share at 1/2 of the decedent's money and property with certain adjustments, or at 1/3 if the decedent left at least 2 descendants not also related to a surviving spouse. Ohio Revised Code 2106.01. <u>To avoid a spouse wanting to use the Elective Share most people give over 1/2 their things to any spouse of theirs (including any family house)</u>.

USING RIGHTS A SPOUSE OFTEN CAN GET THE HOMESTEAD

<u>Many states give a surviving spouse or young children some right to get (or stay in for years) a home owned by a decedent under what is called a "Homestead Law"</u>. Ohio law is unusual and gives family no right to get the homestead. But Ohio law makes clear a spouse using an Elective Share or, also the Allowance for Support (see above) can use these to claim some or all of ownership of decedent's house. Ohio Revised Code 2106.10. Ohio law also basically says creditors can't seek payment from decedent's house unless equity is over $125,000. Of course a normal mortgage later can be foreclosed if not paid monthly. Under Ohio law a surviving spouse no matter what can always stay at a homestead for 1 year. Due to all this <u>most people give a spouse or if no spouse any minor children a house by Will or by other ways (like putting them on the land title)</u>. Of course often spouses do papers such as a deed to hold a house "jointly" so upon the death of one spouse it automatically legally goes to the other.

CHILD ISSUES

WILL CAN NAME "GUARDIAN OF THE PERSON" TO CARE FOR YOUNG CHILD

If a parent dies with a child under age 18 then any other natural or adopted parent (but not a step-parent) almost always automatically gets control of the child's care (including health care, school, and home issues). This won't occur only if the other parent will be unavailable a long time or is proven unfit in court which is rare. But just in case it is later needed (like later both parents die) <u>a Will often names a healthy willing relative or friend as "Guardian of the Person" to give this care for a young child</u>.

WILL CAN NAME "GUARDIAN OF THE ESTATE" FOR CHILD'S PROPERTY

Since a child till age 18 can't legally control property and money <u>a Will often names a person to have the job of managing a young child's property and money</u>. This is called a "Guardian of the Estate", though some other states often call this a "Conservator" or a "Guardian of Property". The Guardian of the Estate will later decide each year how to use up property and money on a child's costs (like school, living, and health care) till often age 18 when all left goes to a child. A judge often holds a yearly hearing to review spending. A person paying stuff for a child can ask to be paid back from a child's resources. As a nice second option most Wills say an Executor may name a person as "Custodian" (including themselves) to manage a child's money and property under the "Uniform Transfers To Minors Act" law and this may avoid a lot of work and costs.

MOST WILLS NAME 1 PERSON TO CARE FOR A CHILD AND A CHILD'S THINGS

This book's Will forms and most parents <u>name the same 1 person</u> to be Guardian of the Person caring for a child and Guardian of the Estate caring for a child's property and money. People can change a Will to name different people for the 2 positions, but this is rarely worth it since parents dying is rare, rarely does a child get much, a person smart enough to handle a child often can handle money, and naming different people can lead to arguments and lawsuits between Guardians. Will gifts <u>can</u> go to someone named to be a Guardian.

PERSON TO HELP A CHILD MUST BE AT LEAST 18

A person to be a Guardian of any kind a person must be at least age 18. They must not have a bad criminal record like a felony unless a judge later says they can serve anyway. They need not live in Ohio but being local can make work easier. The choice for a position of the last living parent is usually followed. If no Will names a person for a position or they're unavailable a judge can pick someone, but family may argue about who to suggest. Naming 2 people for 1 position <u>to act at the same time</u> is rare since 2 persons may argue and any 1 person picked should be smart enough to act alone. It is somewhat common for 2 people who are a married couple to be named for a position, but there can still be problems if they disagree on what to do or if they divorce. Some Wills add a 2nd person to serve <u>if the 1st person is unavailable</u>, like: "or if they are later reasonably unable to serve I name ____ to serve"). But most people skip naming a fallback person since it's rarely needed, if a problem is seen a Will can be redone, and a judge always can pick someone.

NAMING GUARDIANS RARELY MATTERS

A child under age 18 having parents die is rare so parents shouldn't worry that much about Guardians for children. A good U.S. study found of people under age 18 just 2.78% had lost 1 parent and just 0.13% had lost 2 parents (so 99.87% will not lose both parents by age 18). *Parent Mortality Census SIPP Paper #288.*

CHILD ISSUES

WILL CAN NAME "GUARDIAN OF THE PERSON" TO CARE FOR YOUNG CHILD

If a parent dies with a child under age 18 then any other natural or adopted parent (but not a step-parent) almost always automatically gets control of the child's care (including health care, school, and home issues). This won't occur only if the other parent will be unavailable a long time or is proven unfit in court which is rare. But just in case it is later needed (like later both parents die) a Will often names a healthy willing relative or friend as "Guardian of the Person" to give this care for a young child.

WILL CAN NAME "GUARDIAN OF THE ESTATE" FOR CHILD'S PROPERTY

Since a child till age 18 can't legally control property and money a Will often names a person to have the job of managing a young child's property and money. This is called a "Guardian of the Estate", though some other states often call this a "Conservator" or a "Guardian of Property". The Guardian of the Estate will later decide each year how to use up property and money on a child's costs (like school, living, and health care) till often age 18 when all left goes to a child. A judge often holds a yearly hearing to review spending. A person paying stuff for a child can ask to be paid back from a child's resources. As a nice second option most Wills say an Executor may name a person as "Custodian" (including themselves) to manage a child's money and property under the "Uniform Transfers To Minors Act" law and this may avoid a lot of work and costs.

MOST WILLS NAME 1 PERSON TO CARE FOR A CHILD AND A CHILD'S THINGS

This book's Will forms and most parents name the same 1 person to be Guardian of the Person caring for a child and Guardian of the Estate caring for a child's property and money. People can change a Will to name different people for the 2 positions, but this is rarely worth it since parents dying is rare, rarely does a child get much, a person smart enough to handle a child often can handle money, and naming different people can lead to arguments and lawsuits between Guardians. Will gifts <u>can</u> go to someone named to be a Guardian.

PERSON TO HELP A CHILD MUST BE AT LEAST 18

A person to be a Guardian of any kind a person must be at least age 18. They must not have a bad criminal record like a felony unless a judge later says they can serve anyway. They need not live in Ohio but being local can make work easier. The choice for a position of the last living parent is usually followed. If no Will names a person for a position or they're unavailable a judge can pick someone, but family may argue about who to suggest. Naming 2 people for 1 position to act at the same time is rare since 2 persons may argue and any 1 person picked should be smart enough to act alone. It is somewhat common for 2 people who are a married couple to be named for a position, but there can still be problems if they disagree on what to do or if they divorce. Some Wills add a 2nd person to serve if the 1st person is unavailable, like: "or if they are later reasonably unable to serve I name _____ to serve"). But most people skip naming a fallback person since it's rarely needed, if a problem is seen a Will can be redone, and a judge always can pick someone.

NAMING GUARDIANS RARELY MATTERS

A child under age 18 having parents die is rare so parents shouldn't worry that much about Guardians for children. A good U.S. study found of people under age 18 just 2.78% had lost 1 parent and just 0.13% had lost 2 parents (so 99.87% will not lose both parents by age 18). *Parent Mortality Census SIPP Paper #288.*

CHAPTER 6
BASIC IDEAS ABOUT CONTROLLING HEALTH CARE

BASIC IDEAS HELP PEOPLE UNDERSTAND CONTROLLING HEALTH CARE

Some ideas help people understand health care forms.

■ By law people control their own health care by telling doctors and others what they want unless they're "incapacitated" by insufficient ability to a) communicate verbally or by notes, b) be rational, or c) be conscious. In actuality most people keep control of health care till death or till no big treatment options remain, but people may worry they may be incapacitated a long time so they want to do health care forms.

■ If an adult 18 or older becomes incapacitated the adult's closest family like spouse or adult child can make emergency decisions but they usually must then rush to a judge to get further power if no legal document gives them full power over health care.

■ In forms a person can be named to have control of health care if needed who is often called "Agent". Forms about control of health care if people are later incapacitated are often called "Advanced Directives".

■ In forms people can give written health care instructions doctors, family, Agent, and others must obey.

■ Parents do have power over health care of their child under age 18.

■ Some **young married people** give a spouse power over health care in case they are ever incapacitated. Some **young adults** give this power to parents. **Young people** are less often ill so often skip doing things.

■ Pain relief like pain drugs and comfort care is usually given even if forms say to stop or limit other care.

■ Most people only do a single long health care form that has a spot to give someone power over health care and a spot for instructions (this is often called a "Health Care Power of Attorney" though names vary).

■ For the rare times stopping health care ("pulling the plug") likely matters due to extreme illness or old age:

-- most people do nothing special and trust family or Agent for health care to decide on stopping care based on many factors like pain, cost, hassle, suffering and time of treatment, beliefs, and chances of recovery;

-- a few people do a serious document to say to stop most health care if later doctors decide a person is incapacitated, has an irrevocable terminal condition or likely won't regain good consciousness, and more medical care won't help (this document to stop care is often called a "Living Will" though names vary);

-- a few people do a serious document to starting immediately block certain health care (and this often is called a "Do-Not-Resuscitate" if about resuscitation or called a "Physician's Order" if about many treatments).

CHAPTER 7
FORM 1: WILL (STANDARD)

FORM 1 IS A STANDARD WILL THAT IS FLEXIBLE AND WITHOUT A GUARDIAN

Form 1 is a standard Will that is flexible and lets a person control many different things after their death. This is usually also called a "Last Will And Testament". This form is meant for people without a young child.

THIS FORM IS A WILL WITH SEVERAL PARTS

The form starts with lines for a person to put their name (a full legal name is best but not required) and place of main residence (most put a county but some put a city). The Will is still valid if people later move.

Paragraph 1, "List Of Spouse And Children", lets a person write the names of any living spouse and children they have, or if none maybe write "none". This helps show a Testator has enough mental ability and memory to do a Will.

Paragraph 2, "Gifts", has many spaces to make either specific gifts of particular property or general gifts like of money. People can delete, copy and paste to add more, or leave blank these gift lines.

Paragraph 3, "Separate Writings", says to follow any separate writings done apart from the Will that gifts tangible personal property in manner allowed by state law.

Paragraph 4, "Residue", has a Residue Clause to say property and money left after other Will parts and other transfers is to be distributed in the way a person wrote in the blank parts of this paragraph.

Paragraph 5, "Administration", names a person to be Executor to do things after a person's death (many people use the similar term of "Personal Representative" for this).

Paragraph 6, "Miscellaneous", has paragraphs of legal language to help avoid certain legal issues.

Last is paragraphs for Testator to date, sign, and print their name, and for the witnesses to sign, date, and put their addresses.

USUAL RESIDUE CLAUSE HAS 2 PLACES TO NAME PERSONS TO GET THINGS

In a Will "Residue Clause" anything left over after other Will parts is transferred as the clause directs. Many people use a Residue Clause to gift most their things. In this Will form's Residue Clause there is:

1) a 1st space to name 1 or more persons to get the Residue, and if any named here have died before the Will maker then other persons named here in this 1st space take the dead person's share, and

2) a 2nd space to name people to get things if all people named in the 1st space have died, and if any people named in the 2nd space have died their shares go to "lineal descendants" like their children.

People often put in the 1st space a spouse or close family or friends, and in 2nd space next closest people.

TESTATOR AND 2 OR MORE WITNESSES WHILE TOGETHER SIGN WILL

This Will after being filled out (except parts intentionally left blank) must be signed by the person doing the Will (the "Testator") in front of at least 2 persons acting as witnesses at least age 18 who then also sign. Witnesses usually should not be persons named to get anything in the Will or benefit somehow from the Will. In Ohio some people modify a Will to have more than the minimum 2 witnesses to make work easier later, and some Wills are modified to have 4 witnesses. Once completed a Will should be put in a safe place.

LAST WILL AND TESTAMENT

I, _____, of _____, Ohio, do revoke all prior Wills and testamentary documents and do make, publish, and declare this as my Will. I am of sound mind and under no duress or undue influence and acting voluntarily.

1. LIST OF SPOUSE AND CHILDREN. To help show I am mentally competent and have sufficient memory to make a Will I wish to list any living spouse and living children I now have. I currently have the following living spouse and living children:
_____
_____.

2. GIFTS. I give these gifts in this Will, but to get a gift in this section the recipient must survive me except as otherwise stated below.

I give _____ to _____.
I give _____ to _____.
I give _____ to _____.
I give _____ to _____.
I give _____ to _____.
I give _____ to _____.
I give _____ to _____.
I give _____ to _____.

3. SEPARATE WRITINGS. I may do writings separate from this Will to gift tangible personal property as allowed by state law, and all such writings should be followed. But any such writing not found within 90 days of my death is canceled and has no effect. A gift in such a writing to a person who does not survive me is canceled and has no effect. This Will does not revoke any such writings that now exist.

4. RESIDUE. I give the rest and residue and remainder of my estate, my money and property of any kind and nature, and anything I have an interest in so long as it was not transferred by other Will provisions (all of which is called the "residue"), as follows:
  a) to _____ who survive me with persons just named who survive me taking the share of non-survivors, then only if things remain
  b) to _____ and if any of those just named do not survive me their part goes to their lineal descendants per stirpes.

5. ADMINISTRATION. I name, nominate, and appoint _____ as Executor including for me, my Will, and my estate.

6. MISCELLANEOUS. The following applies to this Will and generally.

In this Will no part left unfilled is a mistake including spaces in the residue clause.

The facts support and I want Ohio state law to apply to this Will and my estate.

I order that my just debts, funeral and related expenses, and taxes be paid as soon after my death as practical but only the items my Executor or Personal Representative chooses.

Priority of Will gifts of the same type is based on the order they are written.

If a gift or section in this Will reasonably mentions survival in any way then such survival is an absolute condition and anti-lapse laws or similar have no effect.

The words "give" and "gift" also means a devise, bequest, grant, legacy, or similar.

A gift of property no longer owned by me at death shall lapse and be of no effect including no payment of money shall be done in its place.

Unless a Will gift specifies otherwise if a Will gift goes to multiple recipients if any do not survive me the part to them lapses and instead goes to other surviving recipients.

I am intentionally not providing by Will or other ways for some family, including I am not providing for some children of mine and also children of a deceased child of mine.

No earlier transfer reduces a Will gift unless I usually called it a loan or advancement.

Unless another meaning is shown use of plural includes the singular and vice versa, "they" can mean 1 person, and masculine, feminine, and neuter words are interchangeable.

Unless a Will specifically says otherwise a) a secured debt including a mortgage or lien shall not be paid off including by a Executor or similar or in probate, b) a recipient of a Will gift of property takes it subject to debts, and c) no recipient of property who later loses it or who pays to keep it may require others or the estate to pay or do exoneration.

I request and authorize any informal, summary, and quick probate or similar action. Any Executor or Personal Representative may act independently with no court supervision, including independent administration, and with no inventory, appraisal, or other action.

I give any Executor or Personal Representative the a) fullest authority, discretion, and powers allowed by state law, b) power to lease, sell, mortgage, convey, or keep property including real property in a manner and time they deem helpful or proper, and c) authority to settle or pay claims or debts in the time and manner they in their sole discretion choose.

Any Executor or Personal Representative has sole discretion how to divide a gift to several persons, how to carry out a general gift, and how to do a gift to multiple persons.

Pay for any lawyer is what a Executor or Personal Representative agrees to and not a statutory fee or an amount suggested by a county or other local provision.

Any Guardian of any type, Conservator, Custodian, or other person managing a minor's property or money may use or invade the principal and sell property without court action.

If context permits the terms Personal Representative and Executor and Administrator are interchangeable, Guardian of the Estate and Guardian of Property and Conservator and

Custodian are interchangeable, and residue and residuary are interchangeable. Any such person may stand in place and act and have all powers like the others.

The residue includes lapsed or failed gifts, insurance paid to the estate, digital assets, inheritances owed me, and all I had power of appointment or testamentary disposition over.

Any Personal Representative, Executor, Administrator, Guardian of any type like for a person or estate, Conservator, Custodian, and any other fiduciary under this Will or otherwise shall qualify and serve without bond, surety, security, surety bond, or similar.

If evidence does not show it likely a person survived me by 120 hours (5 days) then for this Will and my estate they shall be deemed in all ways as having died before me.

If part of this Will is by law invalid or unenforceable other provisions remain in effect.

Any Executor or Personal Representative may at any time transfer money or property of a minor under age 18 to a Custodian to serve under the Ohio Uniform Transfers to Minors Act or a similar law anywhere, and may pick the person to be Custodian including they may pick themselves.

TESTATOR

IN WITNESS WHEREOF, I, _____, sign, publish, and declare this instrument as my Will, this ___ day of _____, 20__.

_____
Signature of Testator

WITNESSES

The foregoing instrument was signed by the Testator and Testator declared it to be the Testator's Will, which signing and declaration was made in the presence of us the witnesses, and we do now sign our names in this document below as witnesses at the request and in the presence of the Testator and presence of each other on this the ___ day of _____, 20___.

_____   _____
Signature of Witness   Address of Witness

_____   _____
Signature of Witness   Address of Witness

CHAPTER 8
FORM 2: WILL (GUARDIANS)

FORM 2 IS BASIC WILL WITH GUARDIANS CLAUSE FOR YOUNG CHILD
Form 2 is a Will with a Guardians part to be used by a person with a minor child under age 18.

FORM IS A WILL WITH SEVERAL PARTS INCLUDING A GUARDIAN PART
The form starts with lines for a person to put their name (a full legal name is best but not required) and place of main residence (most put a county but some put a city). The Will is still valid if people later move.

Paragraph 1, "List Of Spouse And Children", lets a person write the names of any living spouse and children they have, or if none maybe write "none". This helps show a Testator has enough mental ability and memory to do a Will and did not just forget they had a spouse or children.

Paragraph 2, "Gifts", has many spaces to make either specific gifts of particular property or general gifts like of money. People can delete, copy and paste to add more, or leave blank these gift lines.

Paragraph 3, "Separate Writings", says to follow any separate writings done apart from the Will that gifts tangible personal property in manner allowed by state law.

Paragraph 4, "Residue", has a Residue Clause to say property and money left after other Will parts and other transfers is to be distributed in the way a person wrote in the blank parts of this paragraph.

Paragraph 5, "Administration", names a person to be Executor to do things after a person's death (many people use the similar term of "Personal Representative" for this).

<u>**Paragraph 6, "Guardians"**, names a person to be if needed Guardian of the Person to care for any minor child under 18, and also to be Guardian of the Estate to manage a minor child's property and money.</u>

Paragraph 7, "Miscellaneous", has paragraphs of legal language to help avoid certain legal issues.

Last is paragraphs for Testator to date and sign, and for the witnesses to sign, date, and put addresses.

USUAL RESIDUE CLAUSE HAS 2 PLACES TO NAME PERSONS TO GET THINGS
In a Will "Residue Clause" anything left over after other Will parts is transferred as the clause directs. Many people use a Residue Clause to gift most their things. In this Will form's Residue Clause there is:

1) a 1st space to name 1 or more persons to get the Residue, and if any named here have died before the Will maker then other persons named here in this 1st space take the dead person's share, and

2) a 2nd space to name people to get things if all people named in the 1st space have died, and if any people named in the 2nd space have died their shares go to "lineal descendants" like their children.

People often put in the 1st space a spouse or close family or friends, and in 2nd space next closest people.

TESTATOR AND 2 OR MORE WITNESSES WHILE TOGETHER SIGN WILL
This Will after being filled out (except parts intentionally left blank) must be signed by the person doing the Will (the "Testator") in front of at least 2 persons acting as witnesses at least age 18 who then also sign. Witnesses usually should not be persons named to get anything in the Will or benefit somehow from the Will. In Ohio some people modify a Will to have more than the minimum 2 witnesses to make work easier later, and some Wills are modified to have 4 witnesses. Once completed a Will should be put in a safe place.

LAST WILL AND TESTAMENT

I, _____, of _____, Ohio, do revoke all prior Wills and testamentary documents and do make, publish, and declare this as my Will. I am of sound mind and under no duress or undue influence and acting voluntarily.

1. LIST OF SPOUSE AND CHILDREN. To help show I am mentally competent and have sufficient memory to make a Will I wish to list any living spouse and living children I now have. I currently have the following living spouse and living children:
_____
_____.

2. GIFTS. I give these gifts in this Will, but to get a gift in this section the recipient must survive me except as otherwise stated below.

I give _____ to _____.
I give _____ to _____.
I give _____ to _____.
I give _____ to _____.
I give _____ to _____.
I give _____ to _____.

3. SEPARATE WRITINGS. I may do writings separate from this Will to gift tangible personal property as allowed by state law, and all such writings should be followed. But any such writing not found within 90 days of my death is canceled and has no effect. A gift in such a writing to a person who does not survive me is canceled and has no effect. This Will does not revoke any such writings that now exist.

4. RESIDUE. I give the rest and residue and remainder of my estate, my money and property of any kind and nature, and anything I have an interest in so long as it was not transferred by other Will provisions (all of which is called the "residue"), as follows:
  a) to _____ who survive me with persons just named who survive me taking the share of non-survivors, then only if things remain
  b) to _____ and if any of those just named do not survive me their part goes to their lineal descendants per stirpes.

5. ADMINISTRATION. I name, nominate, and appoint _____ as Executor including for me, my Will, and my estate.

6. GUARDIANS. I name, nominate, and appoint _____
to be if needed the Guardian of the Person of any minor child under age 18 of mine and to have care, authority, custody, and other control over them. I also name, nominate, and appoint this same person to be Guardian of the Estate over the property, money, and estate of any minor child and to have control, care, and power over these things.

7. MISCELLANEOUS. The following applies to this Will and generally.

In this Will no part left unfilled is a mistake including spaces in the residue clause.

The facts support and I want Ohio state law to apply to this Will and my estate.

I order that my just debts, funeral and related expenses, and taxes be paid as soon after my death as practical but only the items my Executor or Personal Representative chooses.

Priority of Will gifts of the same type is based on the order they are written.

If a gift or section in this Will reasonably mentions survival in any way then such survival is an absolute condition and anti-lapse laws or similar have no effect.

The words "give" and "gift" also means a devise, bequest, grant, legacy, or similar.

A gift of property no longer owned by me at death shall lapse and be of no effect including no payment of money shall be done in its place.

Unless a Will gift specifies otherwise if a Will gift goes to multiple recipients if any do not survive me the part to them lapses and instead goes to other surviving recipients.

I am intentionally not providing by Will or other ways for some family, including I am not providing for some children of mine and also children of a deceased child of mine.

No earlier transfer reduces a Will gift unless I usually called it a loan or advancement.

Unless another meaning is shown use of plural includes the singular and vice versa, "they" can mean 1 person, and masculine, feminine, and neuter words are interchangeable.

Unless a Will specifically says otherwise a) a secured debt including a mortgage or lien shall not be paid off including by a Executor or similar or in probate, b) a recipient of a Will gift of property takes it subject to debts, and c) no recipient of property who later loses it or who pays to keep it may require others or the estate to pay or do exoneration.

I request and authorize any informal, summary, and quick probate or similar action. Any Executor or Personal Representative may act independently with no court supervision, including independent administration, and with no inventory, appraisal, or other action.

I give any Executor or Personal Representative the a) fullest authority, discretion, and powers allowed by state law, b) power to lease, sell, mortgage, convey, or keep property including real property in a manner and time they deem helpful or proper, and c) authority to settle or pay claims or debts in the time and manner they in their sole discretion choose.

Any Executor or Personal Representative has sole discretion how to divide a gift to several persons, how to carry out a general gift, and how to do a gift to multiple persons.

Pay for any lawyer is what a Executor or Personal Representative agrees to and not a statutory fee or an amount suggested by a county or other local provision.

Any Guardian of any type, Conservator, Custodian, or other person managing a minor's

property or money may use or invade the principal and sell property without court action.

If context permits the terms Personal Representative and Executor and Administrator are interchangeable, Guardian of the Estate and Guardian of Property and Conservator and Custodian are interchangeable, and residue and residuary are interchangeable. Any such person may stand in place and act and have all powers like the others.

The residue includes lapsed or failed gifts, insurance paid to the estate, digital assets, inheritances owed me, and all I had power of appointment or testamentary disposition over.

Any Personal Representative, Executor, Administrator, Guardian of any type like for a person or estate, Conservator, Custodian, and any other fiduciary under this Will or otherwise shall qualify and serve without bond, surety, security, surety bond, or similar.

If evidence does not show it likely a person survived me by 120 hours (5 days) then for this Will and my estate they shall be deemed in all ways as having died before me.

If part of this Will is by law invalid or unenforceable other provisions remain in effect.

Any Executor or Personal Representative may at any time transfer money or property of a minor under age 18 to a Custodian to serve under the Ohio Uniform Transfers to Minors Act or a similar law anywhere, and may pick the person to be Custodian including they may pick themselves.

TESTATOR

IN WITNESS WHEREOF, I, _____, sign, publish, and declare this instrument as my Will, this ___ day of _____, 20__.

_____
Signature of Testator

WITNESSES

The foregoing instrument was signed by the Testator and Testator declared it to be the Testator's Will, which signing and declaration was made in the presence of us the witnesses, and we do now sign our names in this document below as witnesses at the request and in the presence of the Testator and presence of each other on this the ____ day of _____, 20___.

_____ _____
Signature of Witness   Address of Witness

_____ _____
Signature of Witness   Address of Witness

CHAPTER 9
FORM 3: HEALTH CARE POWER OF ATTORNEY

FORM CAN NAME HEALTH CARE AGENT AND GIVE INSTRUCTIONS

This form lets a person name someone as "Health Care Agent" to make health care decisions if the person is ever later incapacitated, and if wanted also lets a person write some health care instructions. Many people do this 1 health care form and skip other health care forms. Paramedics or similar people in a hurry usually are too busy to read this long form. At end of the form is a "Notice" about the form for the person doing the form to read.

CAN NAME "AGENT" TO HAVE POWER OVER HEALTH CARE

This form lets a Health Care Agent be named to have power to make medical decisions if the person is ever incapacitated. Often named as Agent is a spouse, adult child, relative, or friend. Naming a family member like a spouse or adult child as Agent can avoid them having to rush to see a judge to get more power in a medical emergency. The form has a spot to name an "Alternate Agent" but many people do not bother since this is rarely needed. To be Agent a person must be at least 18, and they can't work at any place giving health care unless they are a relative or member of the same religious order as the person.

CAN GIVE HEALTH CARE INSTRUCTIONS

In the form a person can write health care instructions that an Agent, family, and doctors should all follow. But many people skip instructions since they are hard to do to cover all medical situations, any instructions can cause delay or lawsuits if not clear, and people trust family or Agent to make wise decisions. Family and any Agent must follow any instructions and in areas without instructions they can use their judgment to do what a person probably would want. People can name an Agent but skip instructions, or write instructions but skip an Agent. Most people initial a spot in the form so an Agent can decline artificial fluids and feeding if they think it best. After doing this form a person with mental capacity is free to override it, like by saying, "My Agent no longer has power and I want all possible health care".

SIGN FORM WITH 2 WITNESSES OR WITH A NOTARY

To do the form a person can either sign with 2 witnesses who then also sign, or they can use a notary. To be a witness a person must be at least 18, not be named Agent in the form, not work at a place giving health care, and not be related to the person by blood, marriage, or adoption. A person can keep the signed form until needed or give it to the Agent or family members to use if needed. The form usually should be quickly shown to any doctor or health care facility that may give care to make it part of person's medical file. To cancel the form a person should tell the Agent and then usually also tell any place that saw the form about the cancellation.

STATE OF OHIO
HEALTH CARE POWER OF ATTORNEY

I, _____, am an adult of sound mind who resides in _____ County, Ohio. I knowingly and voluntarily make this Health Care Power of Attorney as principal.

AUTHORITY OF AGENT. If my physician determines I have lost the capacity to make informed health care decisions my agent named below is given authority to make all physical and mental health care decisions for me, including the right to give, to refuse to give, or to withdraw informed consent to any health care treatment, to the extent allowed by law. My agent shall decide issues consistent with my instructions and other statements written in this document, or for other issues shall act based on things I have made known verbally or in other writings. Subject to other terms of this document my agent shall act in my best interest as determined by considering benefits, burdens, and risks that might result from a given decision. If no agent is available this document will guide decisions about my health care.

AGENT. I hereby name below my agent who will make health care decisions for me as authorized in this document.

Agent's Name: _____
Agent's Address: _____
Agent's Phone And Other Contacts: _____

ALTERNATE AGENT (OPTIONAL). Should the agent named above not be reasonably available, willing, or able to make decisions for me I name the following person as my agent to make health care decisions as authorized in this document. A statement by my alternate agent that they are acting properly may be relied upon without investigation.

Agent's Name: _____
Agent's Address: _____
Agent's Phone And Other Contacts: _____

TIMING. This document is effective immediately, has no expiration date, and shall not be affected by my disability or by the passage of time.

HEALTH CARE INSTRUCTIONS (OPTIONAL). I instruct my agent, physicians, and all other persons to consider the health care treatment instructions and preferences I give below or on attached pages (attach pages if needed): _____
_____
_____
_____
_____

ARTIFICIAL NUTRITION AND HYDRATION AND SIMILAR TREATMENT.

_____ BY PLACING MY INITIALS ON THE LINE IMMEDIATELY TO THE LEFT I HEREBY SPECIFICALLY AUTHORIZE MY AGENT TO REFUSE OR TO WITHDRAW CONSENT TO THE PROVISION OF ARTIFICIAL OR TECHNOLOGICALLY SUPPLIED NUTRITION AND HYDRATION IF I AM IN A PERMANENTLY UNCONSCIOUS STATE AND MY PHYSICIAN AND ANOTHER PHYSICIAN WHO HAS EXAMINED ME DETERMINE TO A REASONABLE DEGREE OF MEDICAL CERTAINTY THAT SUCH NUTRITION OR HYDRATION WILL NOT PROVIDE COMFORT TO ME OR ALLEVIATE MY PAIN.

GUARDIAN. I intend authority given to my agent to eliminate the need for a court to appoint a guardian of my person, however if such proceedings do occur I nominate my agent to serve as the guardian of my person, without bond.

EARLIER DOCUMENTS. Any earlier health care power of attorney or similar documents shall be revoked by this document, but a signed declaration under Ohio Revised Code chapter 2133 (commonly called a "Living Will") is not revoked by this document unless I specifically indicate this here.

COPY AND NOTICE OF REVOCATION. A copy of this document shall be as valid as the original, and I understand if I revoke this document by notifying my agent either in writing or verbally that such revocation is not effective for third parties including physicians until I or a witness to the revocation notify them.

TWO WITNESSES OR NOTARY. This document is not valid until signed in the presence of either a notary public or two witnesses who meet the law's requirements.

SIGNATURE

I understand the terms and purpose of this Health Care Power of Attorney and I sign my name to it as principal on this ___ day of _____, 20__, at _____ County, Ohio.

_____
Principal

WITNESSES

I attest that the principal signed or acknowledged this Health Care Power Of Attorney in my presence, that the principal appears to be of sound mind and not subject to or under duress, fraud, or undue influence. I also attest that 1) I am not an agent named in this document, 2) I am not the attending physician of the principal, 3) I am not the administrator of a nursing home in which the principal is receiving care, and 4) I am at least age 18 and not related to the principal by blood, marriage or adoption.

Date: _____ Signed: _____

Date: _____ Signed: _____

OR

NOTARY

State of Ohio
County of _____ ss:

On _____, 20___, before me, the undersigned Notary Public, personally appeared _____, known to me or satisfactorily proven to be the person whose name is subscribed to the above Health Care Power of Attorney as the principal, and who has acknowledged that he or she executed this document for the purposes expressed therein. I attest that the principal appears to be of sound mind and not under or subject to duress, fraud or undue influence.

My Commission Expires:_____   Signed: _____
Notary Public

[This following notice is included in this printed form as required by Ohio Revised Code § 1337.17.]

NOTICE TO ADULT EXECUTING THIS DOCUMENT

This is an important legal document. Before executing this document, you should know these facts:

This document gives the person you designate (the attorney in fact) the power to make MOST health care decisions for you if you lose the capacity to make informed health care decisions for yourself. This power is effective only when your attending physician determines that you have lost the capacity to make informed health care decisions for yourself and, notwithstanding this document, as long as you have the capacity to make informed health care decisions for yourself, you retain the right to make all medical and other health care decisions for yourself.

You may include specific limitations in this document on the authority of the attorney in fact to make health care decisions for you.

Subject to any specific limitations you include in this document, if your attending physician determines that you have lost the capacity to make an informed decision on a health care matter, the attorney in fact GENERALLY will be authorized by this document to make health care decisions for you to the same extent as you could make those decisions yourself, if you had the capacity to do so. The authority of the attorney in fact to make health care decisions for you GENERALLY will include the authority to give informed consent, to refuse to give informed consent, or to withdraw informed consent to any care, treatment, service, or procedure to maintain, diagnose, or treat a physical or mental condition.

HOWEVER, even if the attorney in fact has general authority to make health care decisions for you under this document, the attorney in fact NEVER will be authorized to do any of the following:

(1) Refuse or withdraw informed consent to life-sustaining treatment (unless your attending physician and one other physician who examines you determine, to a reasonable degree of medical certainty and in accordance with reasonable medical standards, that either of the following applies:

(a) You are suffering from an irreversible, incurable, and untreatable condition caused by disease, illness, or injury from which (i) there can be no recovery and (ii) your death is likely to occur within a relatively short time if life-sustaining treatment is not administered, and your attending physician additionally determines, to a reasonable degree of medical certainty and in accordance with reasonable medical standards, that there is no reasonable possibility that you will regain the capacity to make informed health care decisions for yourself.

(b) You are in a state of permanent unconsciousness that is characterized by you being irreversibly unaware of yourself and your environment and by a total loss of cerebral cortical functioning, resulting in you having no capacity to experience pain or suffering, and your attending physician additionally determines, to a reasonable degree of medical certainty and in accordance with reasonable medical standards, that there is no reasonable possibility that you will regain the capacity to make informed health care decisions for yourself);

(2) Refuse or withdraw informed consent to health care necessary to provide you with comfort care (except that, if he is not prohibited from doing so under (4) below, the attorney in fact could refuse or withdraw informed consent to the provision of nutrition or hydration to you as described under (4) below). (YOU SHOULD UNDERSTAND THAT COMFORT CARE IS DEFINED IN OHIO LAW TO MEAN ARTIFICIALLY OR TECHNOLOGICALLY ADMINISTERED SUSTENANCE (NUTRITION) OR FLUIDS (HYDRATION) WHEN

ADMINISTERED TO DIMINISH YOUR PAIN OR DISCOMFORT, NOT TO POSTPONE YOUR DEATH, AND ANY OTHER MEDICAL OR NURSING PROCEDURE, TREATMENT, INTERVENTION, OR OTHER MEASURE THAT WOULD BE TAKEN TO DIMINISH YOUR PAIN OR DISCOMFORT, NOT TO POSTPONE YOUR DEATH. CONSEQUENTLY, IF YOUR ATTENDING PHYSICIAN WERE TO DETERMINE THAT A PREVIOUSLY DESCRIBED MEDICAL OR NURSING PROCEDURE, TREATMENT, INTERVENTION, OR OTHER MEASURE WILL NOT OR NO LONGER WILL SERVE TO PROVIDE COMFORT TO YOU OR ALLEVIATE YOUR PAIN, THEN, SUBJECT TO (4) BELOW, YOUR ATTORNEY IN FACT WOULD BE AUTHORIZED TO REFUSE OR WITHDRAW INFORMED CONSENT TO THE PROCEDURE, TREATMENT, INTERVENTION, OR OTHER MEASURE.);

(3) Refuse or withdraw informed consent to health care for you if you are pregnant and if the refusal or withdrawal would terminate the pregnancy (unless the pregnancy or health care would pose a substantial risk to your life, or unless your attending physician and at least one other physician who examines you determine, to a reasonable degree of medical certainty and in accordance with reasonable medical standards, that the fetus would not be born alive);

(4) REFUSE OR WITHDRAW INFORMED CONSENT TO THE PROVISION OF ARTIFICIALLY OR TECHNOLOGICALLY ADMINISTERED SUSTENANCE (NUTRITION) OR FLUIDS (HYDRATION) TO YOU, UNLESS:

(A) YOU ARE IN A TERMINAL CONDITION OR IN A PERMANENTLY UNCONSCIOUS STATE.

(B) YOUR ATTENDING PHYSICIAN AND AT LEAST ONE OTHER PHYSICIAN WHO HAS EXAMINED YOU DETERMINE, TO A REASONABLE DEGREE OF MEDICAL CERTAINTY AND IN ACCORDANCE WITH REASONABLE MEDICAL STANDARDS, THAT NUTRITION OR HYDRATION WILL NOT OR NO LONGER WILL SERVE TO PROVIDE COMFORT TO YOU OR ALLEVIATE YOUR PAIN.

(C) IF, BUT ONLY IF, YOU ARE IN A PERMANENTLY UNCONSCIOUS STATE, YOU AUTHORIZE THE ATTORNEY IN FACT TO REFUSE OR WITHDRAW INFORMED CONSENT TO THE PROVISION OF NUTRITION OR HYDRATION TO YOU BY DOING BOTH OF THE FOLLOWING IN THIS DOCUMENT:

(I) INCLUDING A STATEMENT IN CAPITAL LETTERS OR OTHER CONSPICUOUS TYPE, INCLUDING, BUT NOT LIMITED TO, A DIFFERENT FONT, BIGGER TYPE, OR BOLDFACE TYPE, THAT THE ATTORNEY IN FACT MAY REFUSE OR WITHDRAW INFORMED CONSENT TO THE PROVISION OF NUTRITION OR HYDRATION TO YOU IF YOU ARE IN A PERMANENTLY UNCONSCIOUS STATE AND IF THE DETERMINATION THAT NUTRITION OR HYDRATION WILL NOT OR NO LONGER WILL SERVE TO PROVIDE COMFORT TO YOU OR ALLEVIATE YOUR PAIN IS MADE, OR CHECKING OR OTHERWISE MARKING A BOX OR LINE (IF ANY) THAT IS ADJACENT TO A SIMILAR STATEMENT ON THIS DOCUMENT;

(II) PLACING YOUR INITIALS OR SIGNATURE UNDERNEATH OR ADJACENT TO THE STATEMENT, CHECK, OR OTHER MARK PREVIOUSLY DESCRIBED.

(D) YOUR ATTENDING PHYSICIAN DETERMINES, IN GOOD FAITH, THAT YOU AUTHORIZED THE ATTORNEY IN FACT TO REFUSE OR WITHDRAW INFORMED CONSENT TO THE PROVISION OF NUTRITION OR HYDRATION TO YOU IF YOU ARE IN A PERMANENTLY UNCONSCIOUS STATE BY COMPLYING WITH THE REQUIREMENTS OF (4)(C)(I) AND (II) ABOVE.

(5) Withdraw informed consent to any health care to which you previously consented, unless a change in your physical condition has significantly decreased the benefit of that health care to you, or unless the health care is not, or is no longer, significantly effective in achieving the purposes for which you consented to its use.

Additionally, when exercising his authority to make health care decisions for you, the attorney in fact will have to act consistently with your desires or, if your desires are unknown, to act in your best interest. You may express your desires to the attorney in fact by including them in this document or by making them known to him in another manner.

When acting pursuant to this document, the attorney in fact GENERALLY will have the same rights that you have to receive information about proposed health care, to review health care records, and to consent to the disclosure of health care records. You can limit that right in this document if you so choose.

Generally, you may designate any competent adult as the attorney in fact under this document. However, you CANNOT designate your attending physician or the administrator of any nursing home in which you are receiving care as the attorney in fact under this document. Additionally, you CANNOT designate an employee or agent of your attending physician, or an employee or agent of a health care facility at which you are being treated, as the attorney in fact under this document, unless either type of employee or agent is a competent adult and related to you by blood, marriage, or adoption, or unless either type of employee or agent is a competent adult and you and the employee or agent are members of the same religious order. This document has no expiration date under Ohio law, but you may choose to specify a date upon which your durable power of attorney for health care generally will expire. However, if you specify an expiration date and then lack the capacity to make informed health care decisions for yourself on that date, the document and the power it grants to your attorney in fact will continue in effect until you regain the capacity to make informed health care decisions for yourself.

You have the right to revoke the designation of the attorney in fact and the right to revoke this entire document at any time and in any manner. Any such revocation generally will be effective when you express your intention to make the revocation. However, if you made your attending physician aware of this document, any such revocation will be effective only when you communicate it to your attending physician, or when a witness to the revocation or other health care personnel to whom the revocation is communicated by such a witness communicate it to your attending physician.

If you execute this document and create a valid durable power of attorney for health care with it, it will revoke any prior, valid durable power of attorney for health care that you created, unless you indicate otherwise in this document.

This document is not valid as a durable power of attorney for health care unless it is acknowledged before a notary public or is signed by at least two adult witnesses who are present when you sign or acknowledge your signature. No person who is related to you by blood, marriage, or adoption may be a witness. The attorney in fact, your attending physician, and the administrator of any nursing home in which you are receiving care also are ineligible to be witnesses.

If there is anything in this document that you do not understand, you should ask your lawyer to explain it to you.

CHAPTER 10
FORM 4: LIVING WILL DECLARATION

IN FORM CAN SAY STOP MEDICAL CARE IF LATER HEALTH GETS VERY BAD

This form lets a person do the serious act of saying to stop most health care if <u>later</u> the doctors think an incapacitated person has very bad health and more care likely won't help. Paramedics or similar people in a hurry usually are too busy to read this long form.

IN FORM CAN SAY TO NOT GIVE CARE IF LATER HEALTH GETS BAD

This form lets a person say most health care should stop if <u>later</u> the doctors think an incapacitated person has very bad health and more care likely won't help. In Ohio the form basically applies only if 2 doctors agree a person is "<u>permanently unconscious</u>" or has a "<u>terminal condition</u>". The form has the option to cover feeding and water by tube or other artificial means. The form has the option to name persons to contact if a person falls ill, but usually this is left blank as not needed. The form has the option to do Organ Donation but this is usually better done as part of drivers license or state ID forms. After doing the form a person with capacity is free to override it, like by saying, "I want C.P.R. and all care and do now cancel all forms saying different". Hospitals and similar places may have their own form they prefer a person use.

SIGN FORM WITH 2 WITNESSES OR WITH A NOTARY

This form to be valid must be signed by a person with either 2 witnesses or with a person who is a notary. Witnesses must be at least 18, not work for a place providing health care to the person, and not be related by blood, marriage, or adoption to the person doing the form. Once completed the form usually is quickly shown to places that may give care to make it part of person's medical file to be followed. To cancel the form a person should usually tell places that saw the form that it is now canceled.

STATE OF OHIO
LIVING WILL DECLARATION

I, _____, presently residing in _____ County, Ohio, state this is my Ohio Living Will Declaration which I make as its Declarant and wish to be followed by doctors, health care providers, and family. I do this voluntarily to not have my dying be artificially prolonged as explained below. I am of sound mind and not subject to or under duress, fraud, or undue influence. A copy of this document is as good as the original and may be relied upon. This document is effective immediately and has no expiration date. This document may be revoked at any time.

1. IF IN A TERMINAL CONDITION. I may be **unable to make health care decisions while in a terminal condition** (irreversible, incurable, and untreatable condition due to disease, illness, or injury where my physician and another physician after examination agree I cannot recover and death is likely within a reasonably short time without life-sustaining treatment). If such a situation occurs I direct that my physician shall:

   1. Give no or immediately withdraw life-sustaining treatment (meaning any health care that serves mainly to prolong the dying process, including CPR, artificial nutrition and hydration, and anything similar); and

   2. Issue a DNR order (order by physician put in medical records saying no cardiopulmonary resuscitation is to be given); and

   3. Allow me to die naturally and not take action to postpone death, giving only care needed to relieve pain and make me comfortable.

2. IF PERMANENTLY UNCONSCIOUS. I may be **unable to make health care decisions while permanently unconscious** (a nonreversible state where I am permanently unaware of myself and surroundings, and my physician and another physician after examination agree I am unable to feel pain or suffering due to total higher brain function loss). If such a situation occurs I direct that my physician shall:

   1. Give no or immediately withdraw any life-sustaining treatment (meaning any health care that serves mainly to prolong the dying process, including CPR, except artificial nutrition and hydration may continue unless the next paragraph directs otherwise); and

   2. Issue a DNR order (order by physician put in medical records saying no cardiopulmonary resuscitation is to be given); and

   3. Allow me to die naturally and not take action to postpone death, giving only care needed to relieve pain and make me comfortable.

3. **ARTIFICIAL NUTRITION AND HYDRATION.**

_____ BY PLACING MY INITIALS HERE I SPECIFICALLY AUTHORIZE AND INSTRUCT PHYSICIANS TO WITHHOLD OR WITHDRAW ARTIFICIAL OR TECHNOLOGICALLY SUPPLIED NUTRITION AND HYDRATION IF I AM IN A PERMANENTLY UNCONSCIOUS STATE AND MY PHYSICIAN AND ANOTHER PHYSICIAN WHO HAS EXAMINED ME DETERMINE TO A REASONABLE DEGREE OF MEDICAL CERTAINTY THAT SUCH NUTRITION OR HYDRATION WILL NOT PROVIDE COMFORT TO ME OR ALLEVIATE MY PAIN.

4. **PERSONS TO NOTIFY.** If life sustaining treatment will be withheld or withdrawn my physician must use reasonable efforts to notify 1 of the following persons in the following order: a person written below, my guardian, my spouse, my adult child, my parent, or majority of my adult siblings. When trying to notify a person as described above I direct the following persons should first be tried:

Name: _____   Phone: _____

Address: _____

Name: _____   Phone: _____

Address: _____

5. **ANATOMICAL GIFTS (OPTIONAL).** Filing an "Organ Donor Registry Enrollment" form with the Ohio Bureau of Motor Vehicles may be done to make an anatomical gift of all or some of a person's body on death, or several other actions can be taken to do this. A copy of this form is provided with this Living Will Declaration but is optional and need not be used. If a person does not use such a form no presumption is created about intention to make an anatomical gift.

I want to make an anatomical gift: _____   _____
                                                                   Yes   No

SIGNATURE

I understand the purpose, meaning, and effect of this Living Will Declaration which I make as its Declarant and sign my name to on

_____, 20___, at _____, Ohio.

Signed _____

(Either two witnesses or a notary is needed)

WITNESSES

I attest I am at least 18 years old and the above-named Declarant signed or acknowledged the Living Will Declaration in my presence, and to the best of my knowledge appears to be of sound mind and not subject to or under fraud, duress, or undue influence. I also attest I am:
1) not named agent in this person's Health Care Power of Attorney,
2) not attending physician of this person,
3) not administrator of a nursing home the person gets care from, and
4) not related to the person by blood, marriage, or adoption.

Signed: _____   Printed Name: _____

Signed: _____   Printed Name: _____

NOTARY

State of Ohio
County of _____ ss.

On _____, 20___, before me, the undersigned Notary Public, personally appeared _____, known to me or satisfactorily proven to be the person whose name is subscribed to the above Living Will Declaration as the Declarant, and who has acknowledged that he or she executed this document for the purposes expressed therein. I attest that the Declarant appears to be of sound mind and not under or subject to fraud, duress, or undue influence.

My Commission Expires: _____   _____
                                        Signature of Notary Public

CHAPTER 11
FORM 5: DO NOT RESUSCITATE

IN FORM CAN SAY TO IMMEDIATELY NO LONGER TRY C.P.R.

The Do Not Resuscitate form, also called a D-N-R form, lets a person do the serious action of saying to immediately no longer try C.P.R. on them This form is a short 1 page with simple wording that can be read fast by paramedics, EMTs, and similar people that a person may meet outside a hospital or similar. But this form can also be used inside a hospital or similar facility.

FORM IMMEDIATELY STOPS C.P.R. FROM BEING TRIED

This form says to immediately no longer try C.P.R. which is cardio-pulmonary resuscitation to try to restart breathing or the heart. C.P.R. can be painful, cause harm, and be scary to receive or see, and can totally fail or leave a person with chest, brain, or other injuries. Even if this form has been done a sick person can still be taken to get pain relief and comfort care. The D-N-R form must be signed by doctor or similar person, and they usually help a person do this form. Technically in Ohio there is a "non-arrest" and "arrest" version of the form which are similar but let a person say if cardiac arrest (heart stoppage) must occur first. Even after doing form a person with capacity is free to override it, like by not showing paramedics the form or saying loudly a thing like, "I want C.P.R. and ignore my D-N-R". Note, instead of this form many people now do the similar Ohio MOLST form which can cover more kinds of treatment than just C.P.R.

FORM IS SIGNED BY A PERSON'S DOCTOR AND USUALLY THE PERSON

This form must be signed by a person's doctor or similar health professional and usually by the person requesting the form. If a person is incapacitated their Health Care Agent or close family can do the form. Once done the form is usually shown to places that may give care to put in a person's medical file to follow. A person also can keep copies to show to paramedics and similar people who may try to give health care. Or some people wear a "D-N-R bracelet" which a doctor can provide (people should get the "Ohio version"). Helpfully the Ohio D-N-R form has a wallet size form and bracelet size form that can be used instead of just the full size form. To cancel form a person usually should inform all places that were shown the form. People can keep the form secret but most tell family so they explain to health care personnel if needed.

DNR ORDER FORM

A printed copy of this order form or other authorized DNR identification must accompany the patient during transports and transfers between facilities.

Patient Name:	Patient Birth Date:

Optional Patient or Authorized Representatives Signature

Printed name of Physician, APRN or PA*	Date

REQUIRED Signature of Physician, APRN or PA	Phone

REQUIRED for APRN or PA: Name of the supervising physician (PA) or collaborating physician (APRN) for this patient and the physician's NPI, DEA or Ohio medical license number.

CHECK ONLY ONE BOX BELOW

☐ **DNR Comfort Care — Arrest:** Providers will treat patient as any other without a DNR order until the point of cardiac or respiratory arrest at which point all interventions will cease and the DNR Comfort Care protocol will be implemented.

☐ **DNR Comfort Care:** The following DNR protocol is effective immediately.

DNR PROTOCOL

Providers Will:

- Conduct an initial assessment
- Perform Basic Medical Care
- Clear airway of obstruction or suction
- If necessary for comfort or to relieve distress, may administer oxygen, CPAP or BiPAP
- If necessary, may obtain IV access for hydration or pain medication to relieve discomfort, but not to prolong death
- If possible, may contact other appropriate health care providers (hospice, home health, physician, APRN or PA)

Providers Will Not:

- Perform CPR
- Administer resuscitation medications with the intent of restarting the heart or breathing
- Insert an airway adjunct
- De-fibrillate, cardiovert or initiate pacing
- Initiate continuous cardiac monitoring

Physicians, emergency medical services personnel, and persons acting under the direction of or with the authorization of a physician, APRN or PA who participate in the withholding or withdrawal of CPR from the person possessing the DNR identification are provided **immunities under section 2133.22 of the Revised Code.** This DNR order is effective until revoked and may not be altered. Any medical orders, instructions or information other than those required elements of the form itself, that are written on this order form are not transportable and are not provided protections or immunities.

* A DNR may be issued by an Advanced Practice Registered Nurse (APRN) or Physician Assistant (PA) when authorized by section 2133.211 of the Ohio Revised Code.
HEA 1930 Revised 09/01/2019

DNR Comfort Care Wallet Identification Card

❏ DNR Comfort Care ❏ DNR Comfort Care Arrest

Name_____

Birthdate_____ Gender ❏ M ❏ F

Physician name_____

Physician phone_____

Other emergency phone_____

The person named on the front of this card may revoke DNR Comfort Care status by destroying this card.

Hospital Type Bracelet Insert

DNR COMFORT CARE

Name_____ Gender_____

Physician's name_____ Physican's Phone_____

❏ DNRCC ❏ DNRCC—ARREST

CHAPTER 12
FORM 6: STATUTORY FORM POWER OF ATTORNEY

FORM LETS POWER BE GIVEN OVER PROPERTY, MONEY, AND MORE

The form lets a person share power with someone to let them do helpful things with the person's money, property, and more. Some people call this a "Financial Power Of Attorney". This form is a statutory form found in Ohio state law. The form starts with an information page at the start and the end.

FORM GIVES POWER TO LET SOMEONE HELP WITH PROPERTY AND MONEY

This form lets the person doing the form (called the "Principal") give power to someone named in the form (called the "Agent" or "Attorney-in-Fact"). This lets the Agent do things with money, property, and other things of the Principal. Often the Agent is a trusted person like a spouse, relative, or friend. This form can let the Agent do chores, pay bills, move money in accounts, buy or sell items, sign contracts, take out debt, and get information and records from others. This form can help if a person is sick, busy, or away from the state. The form may let a person stay at home, not go to nursing home, and avoid a Conservator or a Guardian. A person with mental capacity can still overrule or fire an Agent, like by saying. Later if an Agent even signs anything it should be like, for example, "Ed Doe signing as Agent under Power of Attorney for Ann Po".

FORM HAS SOME OTHER OPTIONS

In a form powers given can be picked by initialing lines or writing instructions which can cut risk of misuse. But if power given is too limited or unclear then banks and others may not obey an Agent so often much power is given, like by in the form giving "All Preceding Powers". Most people trust the Agent so don't write much. In the form a person can name a "Successor Agent" and a "Guardian", but most people just skip doing this. The form unless modified is "durable" which means it continues even if a person is living but incapacitated.

DUE TO RISKS INCLUDING FRAUD MANY SKIP FORM OR CONSULT A LAWYER

Doing this form can be risky and lead to loss of money and property since an Agent can do dumb or criminal actions like stealing property, wasting money on unneeded items, or being careless. Agents have a legal "duty of care" and can be sued later, but later they might be out of money so can't undo their harm. Usually banks or others can't be blamed for obeying an Agent. Many people ask a lawyer for advice.

IT MAY BE IMPROPER FOR AGENT TO MAKE GIFTS OR DO OTHER THINGS

The law is complex and basic acts of an Agent may be fine like paying bills, moving funds, or getting info, but less usual acts may be improper like doing risky investments or as gifts giving family money or property.

SIGN FORM IN FRONT OF A NOTARY

The form should be signed by person doing it in front of a notary. Once signed the form can be kept by the person till needed or given quickly to the Agent to hold. Some people also show the form quickly to banks or similar places to tell them to later follow it. To cancel the form a person should tell the Agent and take back copies and usually tell people who saw the form it is canceled. Banks and others may later ask an Agent to sign the "affidavit" form found at Ohio Revised Code 1337.61.

STATUTORY FORM POWER OF ATTORNEY

IMPORTANT INFORMATION

This power of attorney authorizes another person (your agent) to make decisions concerning your property for you (the principal). Your agent will be able to make decisions and act with respect to your property (including your money) whether or not you are able to act for yourself. The meaning of authority over subjects listed on this form is explained in the Uniform Power of Attorney Act (sections 1337.21 to 1337.64 of the Revised Code).

This power of attorney does not authorize the agent to make health-care decisions for you.

You should select someone you trust to serve as your agent. Unless you specify otherwise, generally the agent's authority will continue until you die or revoke the power of attorney or the agent resigns or is unable to act for you.

Your agent is entitled to reasonable compensation unless you state otherwise in the Special Instructions.

This form provides for designation of one agent. If you wish to name more than one agent you may name a coagent in the Special Instructions. Coagents are not required to act together unless you include that requirement in the Special Instructions.

If your agent is unable or unwilling to act for you, your power of attorney will end unless you have named a successor agent. You may also name a second successor agent.

This power of attorney becomes effective immediately unless you state otherwise in the Special Instructions.

ACTIONS REQUIRING EXPRESS AUTHORITY

Unless expressly authorized and initialed by me in the Special Instructions, this power of attorney does not grant authority to my agent to do any of the following:
(1) Create a trust;
(2) Amend, revoke, or terminate an inter vivos trust, even if specific authority to do so is granted to the agent in the trust agreement;
(3) Make a gift;
(4) Create or change rights of survivorship;
(5) Create or change a beneficiary designation;
(6) Delegate authority granted under the power of attorney;
(7) Waive the principal's right to be a beneficiary of a joint and survivor annuity, including a survivor benefit under a retirement plan;
(8) Exercise fiduciary powers that the principal has authority to delegate.

CAUTION: Granting any of the above eight powers will give your agent the authority to take actions that could significantly reduce your property or change how your property is distributed at your death.

If you have questions about the power of attorney or the authority you are granting to your agent, you should seek legal advice before signing this form.

DESIGNATION OF AGENT

I, _____ (Name of Principal)
name the following person as my agent:

Name of Agent: _____
Agent's Address: _____
Agent's Telephone Number: _____

DESIGNATION OF SUCCESSOR AGENT(S) (OPTIONAL)

If my agent is unable or unwilling to act for me, I name as my successor agent:

Name of Successor Agent: _____
Successor Agent's Address: _____
Successor Agent's Telephone Number: _____

> If my successor agent is unable or unwilling to act for me, I name as my second successor agent:

Name of Second Successor Agent: _____
Second Successor Agent's Address: _____
Second Successor Agent's Telephone Number: _____

GRANT OF GENERAL AUTHORITY

I grant my agent and any successor agent general authority to act for me with respect to the following subjects as defined in the Uniform Power of Attorney Act (sections 1337.21 to 1337.64 of the Revised Code):

(INITIAL each subject you want to include in the agent's general authority. If you wish to grant general authority over all of the subjects you may initial "All Preceding Subjects" instead of initialing each subject.)

_____ Real Property
_____ Tangible Personal Property
_____ Stocks and Bonds
_____ Commodities and Options
_____ Banks and Other Financial Institutions
_____ Operation of Entity or Business
_____ Insurance and Annuities
_____ Estates, Trusts, and Other Beneficial Interests
_____ Claims and Litigation
_____ Personal and Family Maintenance
_____ Benefits from Governmental Programs or Civil or Military Service
_____ Retirement Plans
_____ Taxes
_____ All Preceding Subjects

LIMITATION ON AGENT'S AUTHORITY

An agent that is not my ancestor, spouse, or descendant MAY NOT use my property to benefit the agent or a person to whom the agent owes an obligation of support unless I have included that authority in the Special Instructions.

SPECIAL INSTRUCTIONS (OPTIONAL)

You may give special instructions on the following lines:

_____
_____
_____
_____
_____
_____
_____
_____
_____

EFFECTIVE DATE

This power of attorney is effective immediately unless I have stated otherwise in the Special Instructions.

NOMINATION OF GUARDIAN (OPTIONAL)

If it becomes necessary for a court to appoint a guardian of my estate or my person, I nominate the following person(s) for appointment:

Name of Nominee for guardian of my estate: _____
Nominee's Address: _____
Nominee's Telephone Number: _____

Name of Nominee for guardian of my person: _____
Nominee's Address: _____
Nominee's Telephone Number: _____

RELIANCE ON THIS POWER OF ATTORNEY

Any person, including my agent, may rely upon the validity of this power of attorney or a copy of it unless that person knows it has terminated or is invalid.

SIGNATURE AND ACKNOWLEDGMENT

_____   _____
Your Signature   Date

_____
Your Name Printed

_____
Your Address

_____
Your Telephone Number

State of Ohio
County of _____
This document was acknowledged before me on _____ (Date),
by _____ (Name of Principal).

_____
Signature of Notary

My commission expires:_____

This document prepared by:
_____

IMPORTANT INFORMATION FOR AGENT

AGENT'S DUTIES

When you accept the authority granted under this power of attorney, a special legal relationship is created between you and the principal. This relationship imposes upon you legal duties that continue until you resign or the power of attorney is terminated or revoked. You must:
(1) Do what you know the principal reasonably expects you to do with the principal's property or, if you do not know the principal's expectations, act in the principal's best interest;
(2) Act in good faith;

(3) Do nothing beyond the authority granted in this power of attorney;

(4) Attempt to preserve the principal's estate plan if you know the plan and preserving the plan is consistent with the principal's best interest;

(5) Disclose your identity as an agent whenever you act for the principal by writing or printing the name of the principal and signing your own name as "agent" in the following manner:

> (Principal's Name) by (Your Signature) as Agent

Unless the Special Instructions in this power of attorney state otherwise, you must also:

(1) Act loyally for the principal's benefit;

(2) Avoid conflicts that would impair your ability to act in the principal's best interest;

(3) Act with care, competence, and diligence;

(4) Keep a record of all receipts, disbursements, and transactions made on behalf of the principal;

(5) Cooperate with any person that has authority to make health-care decisions for the principal to do what you know the principal reasonably expects or, if you do not know the principal's expectations, to act in the principal's best interest.

TERMINATION OF AGENT'S AUTHORITY

You must stop acting on behalf of the principal if you learn of any event that terminates this power of attorney or your authority under this power of attorney. Events that terminate a power of attorney or your authority to act under a power of attorney include:

(1) The death of the principal;

(2) The principal's revocation of the power of attorney or your authority;

(3) The occurrence of a termination event stated in the power of attorney;

(4) The purpose of the power of attorney is fully accomplished;

(5) If you are married to the principal, a legal action is filed with a court to end your marriage, or for your legal separation, unless the Special Instructions in this power of attorney state that such an action will not terminate your authority.

LIABILITY OF AGENT

The meaning of the authority granted to you is defined in the Uniform Power of Attorney Act (sections 1337.21 to 1337.64 of the Revised Code). If you violate the Uniform Power of Attorney Act or act outside the authority granted, you may be liable for any damages caused by your violation.

If there is anything about this document or your duties that you do not understand, you should seek legal advice.

CHAPTER 13
FORM 7: GRANDPARENT POWER OF ATTORNEY

FORM LETS PARENT GIVE POWER TO GRANDPARENT OVER MINOR CHILD

This is a standard form that lets a parent share power over a child under age 18 with a grandparent already watching a child or soon about to. At end of the form is a couple pages of helpful information which are part of the form.

OHIO LETS POWER OVER CHILD GO TO GRANDPARENT WATCHING CHILD

Ohio law lets a parent do this form to share power over a minor child under age 18 with the child's grandparent, but usually only if the grandparent will live with child and parent has some reasonable reason to transfer power (like parent incarceration, lack of funds, drug treatment of any kind, or other good reason). Using this form the grandparent can then control child's health care, activities, schools (enrollment), money, property, and more (but not marriage or adoption). The form is valid for 1 year but can then be renewed. A parent who did the form can cancel it at any time by verbal or written notice to the grandparent or court.

COURT AND OTHER PARENT MUST BE INFORMED IN 5 DAYS

After the form is signed then within 5 days any non-signing parent, the juvenile court where grandparent lives (or other court with jurisdiction), and usually the child's school must get a copy either in person or by certified mail done. Court personnel may require a grandparent do an affidavit with background information and show proof of mailing.

FORM IS SIGNED BY PARENT AND GRANDPARENT IN FRONT OF A NOTARY

The form must be signed in front of a notary by 1 parent (or 2 parents if both sign) and the grandparent given power. The 2nd parent must sign if parents are still married or if there's a shared parenting or custody order, however the 2nd parent need not sign if a) parents are not married and there is no such order, b) if after reasonable efforts the 2nd parent can't be located, c) if paternity is unknown, or d) a court order limits the other parent's rights. Note, in Ohio if a parent can't be located or a court order restricts rights of a parent then a grandparent caring for a child can just sign a "Caretaker Authorization Affidavit" to get power without need for a parent signature.

GRANDPARENT POWER OF ATTORNEY
Ohio Revised Code 3109.53

I, the undersigned, residing at _____, in the county of _____, state of _____, hereby appoint the child's grandparent, _____, residing at _____, in the county of _____, in the state of Ohio, with whom the child of whom I am the parent, guardian, or custodian is residing, my attorney in fact to exercise any and all of my rights and responsibilities regarding the care, physical custody, and control of the child, _____ born _____, having social security number (optional) _____, except my authority to consent to marriage or adoption of the child _____,

and to perform all acts necessary in the execution of the rights and responsibilities hereby granted, as fully as I might do if personally present. The rights I am transferring under this power of attorney include the ability to enroll the child in school, to obtain from the school district educational and behavioral information about the child, to consent to all school-related matters regarding the child, and to consent to medical, psychological, or dental treatment for the child. This transfer does not affect my rights in any future proceedings concerning the custody of the child or the allocation of the parental rights and responsibilities for the care of the child and does not give the attorney in fact legal custody of the child. This transfer does not terminate my right to have regular contact with the child.

I hereby certify that I am transferring the rights and responsibilities designated in this power of attorney because one of the following circumstances exists:
  (1) I am:
    (a) Seriously ill, incarcerated, or about to be incarcerated,
    (b) Temporarily unable to provide financial support or parental guidance to the child,
    (c) Temporarily unable to provide adequate care and supervision of the child because of my physical or mental condition,
    (d) Homeless or without a residence because the current residence is destroyed or otherwise uninhabitable, or
    (e) In or about to enter a residential treatment program for substance abuse;
  (2) I am a parent of the child, the child's other parent is deceased, and I have authority to execute the power of attorney; or
  (3) I have a well-founded belief that the power of attorney is in the child's best interest.

I hereby certify that I am not transferring my rights and responsibilities regarding the child for the purpose of enrolling the child in a school or school district so that the child may participate in the academic or interscholastic athletic programs provided by that school or school district.

I understand that this document does not authorize a child support enforcement agency to redirect child support payments to the grandparent designated as attorney in fact. I further

understand that to have an existing child support order modified or a new child support order issued administrative or judicial proceedings must be initiated.

If there is a court order naming me the residential parent and legal custodian of the child who is the subject of this power of attorney and I am the sole parent signing this document, I hereby certify that one of the following is the case:

(1) I have made reasonable efforts to locate and provide notice of the creation of this power of attorney to the other parent and have been unable to locate that parent;
(2) The other parent is prohibited from receiving a notice of relocation; or
(3) The parental rights of the other parent have been terminated by juvenile court order.

This POWER OF ATTORNEY is valid until the occurrence of whichever of the following events occurs first:

(1) I revoke this POWER OF ATTORNEY in writing and give notice of the revocation to the grandparent designated as attorney in fact and the juvenile court with which this POWER OF ATTORNEY was filed;
(2) the child ceases to reside with the grandparent designated as attorney in fact;
(3) this POWER OF ATTORNEY is terminated by court order;
(4) the death of the child who is the subject of the power of attorney; or
(5) the death of the grandparent designated as the attorney in fact.

WARNING: DO NOT EXECUTE THIS POWER OF ATTORNEY IF ANY STATEMENT MADE IN THIS INSTRUMENT IS UNTRUE. FALSIFICATION IS A CRIME UNDER SECTION 2921.13 OF THE REVISED CODE, PUNISHABLE BY THE SANCTIONS UNDER CHAPTER 2929. OF THE REVISED CODE, INCLUDING A TERM OF IMPRISONMENT OF UP TO 6 MONTHS, A FINE OF UP TO $1,000, OR BOTH.

Witness my hand this _____ day of _____, 20____.

_____   _____
Parent/Custodian/Guardian's signature   Parent's signature

_____
Grandparent designated as attorney in fact

State of Ohio   )
County of _____   ) ss:

Subscribed, sworn to, and acknowledged before me this ___ day of _____, 20___.

_____
Notary Public

NOTICES:

1. A power of attorney may be executed only if one of the following circumstances exists:
(1) The parent, guardian, or custodian of the child is: (a) Seriously ill, incarcerated, or about to be incarcerated; (b) Temporarily unable to provide financial support or parental guidance to the child; (c) Temporarily unable to provide adequate care and supervision of the child because of the parent's, guardian's, or custodian's physical or mental condition; (d) Homeless or without a residence because the current residence is destroyed or otherwise uninhabitable; or (e) In or about to enter a residential treatment program for substance abuse; (2) One of the child's parents is deceased and the other parent, with authority to do so, seeks to execute a power of attorney; or (3) The parent, guardian, or custodian has a well-founded belief that the power of attorney is in the child's best interest.

2. The signatures of the parent, guardian, or custodian of the child and the grandparent designated as the attorney in fact must be notarized by an Ohio notary public.

3. A parent, guardian, or custodian who creates a power of attorney must notify the parent of the child who is not the residential parent and legal custodian of the child unless one of the following circumstances applies: (a) the parent is prohibited from receiving a notice of relocation in accordance with section 3109.051 of the Revised Code of the creation of the power of attorney; (b) the parent's parental rights have been terminated by order of a juvenile court pursuant to Chapter 2151. of the Revised Code; (c) the parent cannot be located with reasonable efforts; (d) both parents are executing the power of attorney. The notice must be sent by certified mail not later than five days after the power of attorney is created and must state the name and address of person designated as attorney in fact.

4. A parent, guardian, or custodian who creates a power of attorney must file it with the juvenile court of the county in which the attorney in fact resides, or any other court that has jurisdiction over the child under a previously filed motion or proceeding. The power of attorney must be filed not later than five days after the date it is created and be accompanied by a receipt showing that the notice of creation of the power of attorney was sent to the parent who is not the residential parent and legal custodian by certified mail.

5. This power of attorney does not affect the rights of the child's parents, guardian, or custodian regarding any future proceedings concerning the custody of the child or the allocation of the parental rights and responsibilities for the care of the child and does not give the attorney in fact legal custody of the child.

6. A person or entity that relies on this power of attorney, in good faith, has no obligation to make any further inquiry or investigation.

7. This power of attorney terminates on the occurrence of whichever of the following occurs first:
(1) the power of attorney is revoked in writing by the person who created it and that person gives written notice of the revocation to the grandparent who is the attorney in fact and the juvenile court with which the power of attorney was filed; (2) the child ceases to live with the grandparent who is the attorney in fact; (3) the power of attorney is terminated by court order; (4) the death of the child who is the subject of the power of attorney; or (5) the death of the grandparent designated as attorney in fact.

If this power of attorney terminates other than by the death of the attorney in fact, the grandparent who served as the attorney in fact shall notify, in writing, all of the following:
(a) Any schools, health care providers, or health insurance coverage provider with which the child has been involved through the grandparent;
(b) Any other person or entity with an ongoing relationship with the child or grandparent such that the other person or entity would reasonably rely on the power of attorney unless notified of the termination;
(c) The court in which the power of attorney was filed after its creation;
(d) The parent who is not the residential parent and legal custodian of the child who is required to be given notice of its creation. The grandparent shall make the notifications not later than one week after the date the power of attorney terminates.

8. If this power of attorney is terminated by written revocation of the person who created it, or the revocation is regarding a second or subsequent power of attorney, a copy of the revocation must be filed with the court with which that power of attorney was filed.

ADDITIONAL INFORMATION:
TO THE GRANDPARENT DESIGNATED AS ATTORNEY IN FACT:

1. If the child stops living with you, you are required to notify, in writing, any school, health care provider, or health care insurance provider to which you have given this power of attorney. You are also required to notify, in writing, any other person or entity that has an ongoing relationship with you or the child such that the person or entity would reasonably rely on the power of attorney unless notified. The notification must be made not later than one week after the child stops living with you.

2. You must include with the power of attorney the following information:
(a) The child's present address, the addresses of the places where the child has lived in last five years, and name and present address of each person whom the child has lived during that period;
(b) Whether you have participated as a party, a witness, or in any other capacity in any other litigation, in this state or any other state, that concerned the allocation, between the parents of the same child, of parental rights and responsibilities for the care of the child and the designation of the residential parent and legal custodian of the child or that otherwise concerned the custody of the same child;
(c) Whether you have information of any parenting proceeding concerning the child pending in a court of this or any other state;
(d) Whether you know of any person who has physical custody of the child or claims to be a parent of the child who is designated the residential parent and legal custodian of the child or to have parenting time rights with respect to the child or to be a person other than a parent of the child who has custody or visitation rights with respect to the child;
(e) Whether you previously have been convicted of or pleaded guilty to any criminal offense involving any act that resulted in a child's being an abused child or a neglected child or previously have been determined, in a case in which a child has been adjudicated an abused child or a neglected child, to be the perpetrator of the abusive or neglectful act that was the basis of the adjudication.

3. If you receive written notice of revocation of the power of attorney or the parent, custodian, or guardian removes the child from your home and if you believe that the revocation or removal is not in the best interest of the child, you may, within fourteen days, file a complaint in the juvenile court to seek custody. You may retain physical custody of the child until the fourteen-day period elapses or, if you file a complaint, until the court orders otherwise.

TO SCHOOL OFFICIALS:

1. Except as provided in section 3313.649 of the Revised Code, this power of attorney, properly completed and notarized, authorizes the child in question to attend school in the district in which the grandparent designated as attorney in fact resides and that grandparent is authorized to provide consent in all school-related matters and to obtain from the school district educational and behavioral information about the child. This power of attorney does not preclude the parent, guardian, or custodian of the child from having access to all school records pertinent to the child.

2. The school district may require additional reasonable evidence the grandparent lives in the district.

3. A school district or school official that reasonably and in good faith relies on this power of attorney has no obligation to make any further inquiry or investigation.

TO HEALTH CARE PROVIDERS:

1. A person or entity that acts in good faith reliance on a power of attorney to provide medical, psychological, or dental treatment, without actual knowledge of facts contrary to those stated in the power of attorney, is not subject to criminal liability or to civil liability to any person or entity, and is not subject to professional disciplinary action, solely for such reliance if the power of attorney is completed and the signatures of the parent, guardian, or custodian of the child and the grandparent designated as attorney in fact are notarized.

2. The decision of a grandparent designated as attorney in fact, based on a power of attorney, shall be honored by a health care facility or practitioner, school district, or school official.

CHAPTER 14
FORM 8: LIMITED POWER OF ATTORNEY OVER CHILD

FORM LETS PARENT SHARE POWER WITH SOMEONE OVER A MINOR CHILD

This form lets a parent share power over a minor child under age 18 with someone named in the form. This book's form is based on a form often used in Ohio if a parent is away due to immigration proceedings. Instead of using this form some people have the local Juvenile Court officially give "temporary custody" of a child to someone for up to 1 year.

FORM CAN DESIGNATE SOMEONE TO SHARE POWER OVER A CHILD

In the form a parent or similar person can name someone as "Attorney-in-Fact" to also have power over the minor child. Often this person given power is called the "Agent". This form can let helpfully let a friend, relative, or teacher make decisions if needed about a child's health care, school, food, home, or discipline. This form might be done if parent is away from child due to work trip, work training, school, sports, drug treatment of any kind, prison or jail, military service, immigration, vacation, visit with family, or if child is sick in hospital and parent must be away like at work. The parent doing the form still has power and can overrule any decision or cancel the form.

COMPLETE FORM BY SIGNING IN FRONT OF NOTARY

The form is completed by 1 or 2 parents signing the form in front of a notary who then notarizes it. To cancel the form a parent should tell the person who got power and take back copies, and they also should usually tell everyone who was shown the form it is cancelled.

LIMITED POWER OF ATTORNEY OVER CHILD
(OVER CHILD, MEDICAL CARE, ACCESS TO EDUCATIONAL RECORDS, AND AUTHORITY TO MAKE EDUCATION DECISIONS)

PARENT / PRINCIPAL
Name:_____
Date of birth:_____
Address: _____
ID or other information:_____

PARENT / PRINCIPAL
Name:_____
Date of birth:_____
Address: _____
ID or other information:_____

CHILD
Name:_____
Date of birth:_____
Address: _____
ID or other information:_____

ATTORNEY-IN-FACT
Name:_____
Date of birth:_____
Address:_____
ID or other information:_____

I/We, _____ and _____, as parent(s) and/or custodian(s) of _____, hereinafter referred to as "child", hereby delegate to _____, hereinafter referred to as my/our "Attorney-in-Fact", the authority to act in my/our place and stead with respect to each of the following powers pursuant to Ohio Revised Code Chapter 1337:

1. To consent to any necessary medical treatment, surgery, medication, therapy, hospitalization or other such care of or for the child;

2. To employ, retain or discharge any person who may care for, counsel, treat or in any manner assist the child;

3. To receive Protected Health Information under the Health Insurance Portability and Accountability Act (HIPAA) about my/our child, including release of records;

4. To obtain copies of my/our child's educational records kept in any of my/our child's educational files. I/we waive and release educational institutions from any restrictions imposed by law in disclosing or revealing any educational record, including the Family Educational Rights and Privacy Act, 20 U.S.C. 1232g and Ohio Revised Code Section 3319.321;

5. To participate in any educational decisions about my/our child as if the designated Attorney-in-Fact herein was a parent or guardian of the child. I/we waive and release educational institutions from any restrictions imposed by law in determining who may make educational decisions for my/our child, including the Family Educational Rights and Privacy Act, 20 U.S.C. 1232g and Ohio Revised Code Chapter 3319;

6. To drop off or pick up my/our child from school or approve travel that is part of my/our child's education. I/we waive and release educational institutions from any restrictions imposed by law in determining who may pick up or drop off my/our child at school or approve travel for educational activities;

7. To exercise the same parental rights I/we may exercise with respect to the care, custody and control of the child and the discretion to exercise the same rights in my/our Attorney-in-Fact's home or any other place selected by my/our Attorney-in-Fact in his/her discretion;

8. To authorize and consent to travel with child to and from the United States of America; and

9. To perform all other acts necessary, or incidental to the execution of the powers enumerated herein.

Any lawful act performed by my/our agent shall be binding upon myself/ourselves, my/our heirs, beneficiaries, personal representatives and assigns. I/We reserve the right to amend or revoke this Limited Power of Attorney at any time hereafter; provided, however, any institution or other party dealing with my agent may rely upon this Limited Power of Attorney until receipt by it of a duly executed copy of my/our revocation thereof.

Any reproduced copy of this signed original shall be deemed to be an original counterpart of this Limited Power of Attorney. This Limited Power of Attorney shall not be affected by any legal incapacity during my/ our lifetime, except as provided by statute.

This Limited Power of Attorney shall remain in effect from date of signing and terminate upon any later written or verbal revocation or 1 year after the date of signing whichever occurs first.

Dated:_____

Signature(s):_____   _____

STATE OF OHIO   )
COUNTY OF   )

On this ___ day of _____, 20___, before me, a Notary Public in and for said County and State, personally came _____ and acknowledged the signing of the foregoing instrument, and that the same is his/her/their voluntary act and deed.

IN TESTIMONY WHEREOF, I have hereunto subscribed my name and affixed my notarial seal on the day and year first above written.

Notary Public Signature:_____
My Commission Expires:_____

CHAPTER 15
FORM 9: DECLARATION FOR FUNERAL ARRANGEMENTS

LETS PERSON BE NAMED TO CONTROL FUNERAL AND RELATED MATTERS
This form lets a person be named to control funeral, burial, cremation, ceremonies, and related matters. This is a statutory form found in Ohio law for people to use if they want.

IN FORM CAN NAME AGENT TO CONTROL FUNERAL AND RELATED MATTERS
This form lets a person doing the form (called "Declarant") name someone (called "Representative") to control their bodily remains after death including related things like burial, cremation, ceremonies, tombstone, related dinners and meetings, and buying things to do all this. If this form is not done then under Oho law the closest family control these things starting with the person's spouse, then adult children, then parents, and then siblings. This form is rarely used and usually is only done if a person's family likely will be too upset while mourning, be bad with money, or do unwanted things.

A PERSON'S WISHES SHOULD BE FOLLOWED AND ESTATE PAYS FOR THINGS
People including family should do things the dead person wanted if their money and property can afford it. Payment for things comes from pre-paid funeral accounts, insurance, and the decedent's or estate's money and property, and Executor and family legally are required to help arrange payment as quickly as possible. The form has a spot to write in instructions but many people skip this and trust their family or person given power to be wise or do what was discussed. Often a person does writes to urge low cost, like for example "Try to spend under $1000 on funeral, skip a gravesite service, use a plain tombstone at Hill Cemetery, and hold a big family dinner in a few months".

SIGN FORM WITH 2 WITNESSES
The form must be signed by a person in front of 2 witness or a notary. Witnesses must be at least 18, not be named Representative in the form, and not be related by blood, marriage, or adoption to the person. There is a spot for the Representative to sign to accept power but this is optional. People should keep the form so it can be found within days of a death. The form can be canceled by saying so or by throwing it away.

DECLARATION FOR FUNERAL ARRANGEMENTS
OHIO REVISED CODE 2108.72

I, _____
(legal name and present address of declarant), an adult being of sound mind, willfully and voluntarily appoint my representative, named below, to have the right of disposition, as defined in section 2108.70 of the Revised Code, for my body upon my death. All decisions made by my representative with respect to the right of disposition shall be binding.

REPRESENTATIVE:
(If the representative is a group of persons, indicate the name, last known address, and telephone number of each person in the group.)

    Name(s): _____
    Address(es): _____
    Telephone Number(s): _____

SUCCESSOR REPRESENTATIVE:
If my representative is disqualified from serving as my representative as described in section 2108.75 of the Revised Code, then I hereby appoint the following person or group of persons to serve as my successor representative.

(If the successor representative is a group of persons, indicate the name, last known address, and telephone number of each person in the group.)

    Name(s): _____
    Address(es): _____
    Telephone Number(s): _____

PREFERENCES
PREFERENCES REGARDING HOW THE RIGHT OF DISPOSITION SHOULD BE EXERCISED, INCLUDING ANY RELIGIOUS OBSERVANCES THE DECLARANT WISHES A REPRESENTATIVE OR A SUCCESSOR REPRESENTATIVE TO CONSIDER:

_____
_____
_____

SOURCES OF FUNDS
ONE OR MORE SOURCES OF FUNDS THAT COULD BE USED TO PAY FOR GOODS AND SERVICES ASSOCIATED WITH AN EXERCISE OF THE RIGHT OF DISPOSITION (REPRESENTATIVE MAY BE ENTITLED TO REIMBURSEMENT FROM THE DECEDENT'S PROBATE ESTATE, ORC 2106.20):

_____
_____

DURATION:
The appointment of my representative and, if applicable, successor representative, becomes effective upon my death.

PRIOR APPOINTMENTS REVOKED:
I hereby revoke any written declaration I executed in accordance with section 2108.70 of the Ohio Revised Code prior to the date of execution of this written declaration indicated below.

AUTHORIZATION TO ACT:
-- Cemetery organization;
-- Crematory operator;
-- Business operating a columbarium;
-- Funeral director;
-- Embalmer;
-- Funeral home;
-- Any other person asked to assist with my funeral, burial, cremation, or other manner of final disposition.

MODIFICATION AND REVOCATION – WHEN EFFECTIVE:
Any modification or revocation of this written declaration is not effective as to any party until that party receives actual notice of the modification or revocation.

LIABILITY:
No person who acts in accordance with a properly executed copy of this written declaration shall be liable for damages of any kind associated with the person's reliance on this declaration.

ACKNOWLEDGMENT OF ASSUMPTION OF OBLIGATIONS AND COSTS:
By signing below, the representative, or successor representative, if applicable, acknowledges that he or she, as representative or successor representative, assumes the right of disposition as defined in section 2108.70 of the Revised Code, and understands that he or she is liable for the reasonable costs of exercising the right, including any goods and services that are purchased.

ACCEPTANCE (OPTIONAL):
The undersigned hereby accepts this appointment as representative or successor representative, as applicable, for the right of disposition as defined in section 2108.70 of the Revised Code.

Signed this _____ day of _____, 20___.

_____
Signature of representative

Signed this ___ day of _____, 20___.

_____
(Signature of declarant)

WITNESSES:
I attest that the declarant signed or acknowledged this assignment of the right of disposition under section 2108.70 of the Revised Code in my presence and that the declarant is at least eighteen years of age and appears to be of sound mind and not under or subject to duress, fraud, or undue influence. I further attest that I am not the declarant's representative or successor representative, I am at least eighteen years of age, and I am not related to the declarant by blood, marriage, or adoption.

First witness:
Name (printed) _____
Residing at: _____
Signature: _____
Date: _____

Second witness:
Name (printed) _____
Residing at: _____
Signature: _____
Date: _____

OR

NOTARY ACKNOWLEDGMENT:

State of Ohio
County of _____ SS.

On _____, before me, the undersigned notary public, personally appeared _____, known to me or satisfactorily proven to be the person whose name is subscribed as the declarant, and who has acknowledged that he or she executed this written declaration under section 2108.70 of the Revised Code for the purposes expressed in that section. I attest that the declarant is at least eighteen years of age and appears to be of sound mind and not under or subject to duress, fraud, or undue influence.

Signature of notary public:_____
My commission expires on: _____

APPENDIX: SAMPLE FILLED OUT FORMS

TO GET FORMS TO USE PEOPLE CAN:
    (1) PHOTOCOPY BOOK PAGES,
    (2) TEAR OUT PAGES FROM A BOOK, OR
    (3) DOWNLOAD BOOK WITH FORMS FROM WWW.DAVENPORTPUBLISHING.COM
AND <u>USUALLY PDF FORM AT IS BEST</u> TO AVOID SPACING/FORMAT CHANGES.

EMAIL ANY COMMENTS TO DAVENPORTPRESS@GMAIL.COM.

On the next pages to show how it can be done are some sample filled out legal forms.

People can add words to legal forms by computer or typewriter to be neater, but many people just by hand use pen, marker, or pencil to handwrite words into forms.

It is not required but is bit better if signatures are in ink or marker not pencil.

Many parts of the forms especially Will gifts can be left empty and unfilled.

Anyone can fill in words in legal form not just the person doing the form, like a friend with neat writing can fill in all the words, addresses, and dates that are needed. <u>Only the final signatures must be done by each person who wants the</u> form.

To add words in form by pen, pencil, typewriter, or computer any of these is fine:
        "I appoint ___*John Doe*___ as Agent",
        "I appoint ___John Doe___ as Agent",
        "I appoint John Doe as Agent".

When doing forms it may help to know "respectively" means "in order just stated".

People need not worry about neatness or small mistakes, and a document is usually fine if those people who knew a decedent in life can tell the likely meaning.

Sample Filled Out Form: Last Will and Testament (Standard) with Gifts section skipped to not bother making small gifts

LAST WILL AND TESTAMENT

I, __Paul Samuel Maxwell__, of __Adams County__, Ohio, do revoke all prior Wills and testamentary documents and do make, publish, and declare this as my Will. I am of sound mind and under no duress or undue influence and acting voluntarily.

1. LIST OF SPOUSE AND CHILDREN. To help show I am mentally competent and have sufficient memory to make a Will I wish to list any living spouse and living children I now have. I currently have the following living spouse and living children:

__none__

2. GIFTS. I give these gifts in this Will, but to get a gift in this section the recipient must survive me except as otherwise stated below.

I give _____ to _____.
I give _____ to _____.
I give _____ to _____.
I give _____ to _____.
I give _____ to _____.
I give _____ to _____.

SKIPPED

3. SEPARATE WRITINGS. I may do writings separate from this Will to gift tangible personal property as allowed by state law, and all such writings should be followed. But any such writing not found within 90 days of my death is canceled and has no effect. A gift in such a writing to a person who does not survive me is canceled and has no effect. This Will does not revoke any such writings that now exist.

4. RESIDUE. I give the rest and residue and remainder of my estate, my money and property of any kind and nature, and anything I have an interest in so long as it was not transferred by other Will provisions (all of which is called the "residue"), as follows:

  a) to __Susan Lee Maxwell my sister__ who survive me with persons just named who survive me taking the share of non-survivors, then if anything remains

  b) to __Oscar David Maxwell and Jennifer Judy Tabor__ and if any of those just named do not survive me their part goes to their lineal descendants, per stirpes.

5. ADMINISTRATION. I nominate and appoint _Susan Lee Maxwell_ as Personal Representative including for me, my Will, and my estate.

6. MISCELLANEOUS. The following applies to this Will and generally.

In this Will no part left unfilled is a mistake including spaces in the residue clause.

The facts support and I want Ohio state law to apply to this Will and my estate.

Priority of Will gifts of the same type is based on the order they are written.

If a gift or section in this Will reasonably mentions survival in any way then such survival is an absolute condition and anti-lapse laws or similar have no effect.

The words "give" and "gift" also means a devise, bequest, grant, legacy, or similar.

A gift of property no longer owned by me at death shall lapse and be of no effect including no payment of money shall be done in its place.

Unless a Will gift specifies otherwise if a Will gift goes to multiple recipients if any do not survive me the part to them lapses and instead goes to other surviving recipients.

I am intentionally not providing by Will or other ways for some family, including I am not providing for some children of mine and also children of a deceased child of mine.

No earlier transfer reduces a Will gift unless I usually called it a loan or advancement.

Unless another meaning is shown use of plural includes the singular and vice versa, "they" can mean 1 person, and masculine, feminine, and neuter words are interchangeable.

Unless a Will specifically says otherwise a) a secured debt including a mortgage or lien shall not be paid off including by a Personal Representative or in probate, b) a recipient of a Will gift of property takes it subject to debts, and c) no recipient of property who later loses it or who pays to keep it may require others or the estate to pay or do exoneration.

I request and authorize any informal, summary, and quick probate or similar action. Any Personal Representative may act independently with no supervision of any court, including independent administration, and with no inventory, appraisal, or other action.

I give any Personal Representative the a) fullest authority, discretion, and powers allowed by state law, b) power to lease, sell, mortgage, convey, or keep property including real property in a manner and time they deem helpful or proper, and c) authority to settle or pay claims or debts in the time and manner they in their sole discretion choose.

Any Personal Representative has sole discretion how to divide a gift to several persons, how to carry out a general gift, and how to do a gift to multiple persons.

Pay for any lawyer is what a Personal Representative agrees to and not a statutory fee.

Any Guardian of any type, Conservator, Custodian, or other person managing a minor's property or money may use or invade the principal and sell property without court action.

If context permits the terms Personal Representative and Executor and Administrator are interchangeable, Guardian of Property and Conservator and Guardian of the Estate and Custodian are interchangeable, and residue and residuary are interchangeable. Any such person may stand in place and act and have all powers like the others.

The residue includes lapsed or failed gifts, insurance paid to the estate, digital assets, inheritances owed me, and all I had power of appointment or testamentary disposition over.

Any Personal Representative, Executor, Administrator, Guardian of any type like for a person or estate, Conservator, Custodian, and any other fiduciary under this Will or otherwise shall qualify and serve without bond, surety, security, surety bond, or similar.

If evidence does not show it likely a person survived me by 120 hours (5 days) then for this Will and my estate they shall be deemed in all ways as having died before me.

If part of this Will is by law invalid or unenforceable other provisions remain in effect.

Any Personal Representative may at any time transfer money or property of a minor under age 18 to a Custodian to serve under the Ohio Uniform Transfers to Minors Act or a similar law anywhere, and may pick the person to be Custodian including themselves.

TESTATOR

IN WITNESS WHEREOF, I, *Paul Samuel Maxwell* , sign, publish, and declare this instrument as my Will, this __22nd__ day of __June__ , 20__22__ .

Paul Samuel Maxwell
Signature of Testator

WITNESSES

The foregoing instrument was signed by the Testator and Testator declared it to be the Testator's Will, which signing and declaration was made in the presence of us the witnesses, and we do now sign our names in this document below as witnesses at the request and in the presence of the Testator and presence of each other on this __22nd__ day of __June__ , 20__22__ .

Nancy Ann Smith　　　　　24 Main St., Bond, OH 43882
Signature of Witness　　　　　Address of Witness

Pamela Bonnie Rooker　　　　　15 Roy St., Bond, OH 43882
Signature of Witness　　　　　Address of Witness

Sample Filled Out Form: Last Will and Testament (Guardian)
with Gifts clause having many gifts, Guardians part used, and Residue Given By Percentages

LAST WILL AND TESTAMENT

I, __Paul Brian Baker__, of __Brown County__, Ohio, do revoke all prior Wills and testamentary documents and do make, publish, and declare this as my Will. I am of sound mind and under no duress or undue influence and acting voluntarily.

1. LIST OF SPOUSE AND CHILDREN. To help show I am mentally competent and have sufficient memory to make a Will I wish to list any living spouse and living children I now have. I currently have the following living spouse and living children:
_____Ruth May Baker wife_____Oscar Elliot Baker young son_____
_____ Karen Lisa Lundy daughter_____ Derek Rupert Baker son _____.

2. GIFTS. I give these gifts in this Will, but to get a gift in this section the recipient must survive me except as otherwise stated below.

I give _____big oak table_____ to _____Anne J. Smith_____.

I give __$5,000 and Ford Truck__ to __Loretta Marsha Baxter__.

I give __buildings, land, and fixtures at 63 Wentworth Road, Columbus, Ohio__ to __Kenneth Alan Ford__.

I give __all real property and fixtures I own in Adams County in Ohio__ to __Amy Marie Fox and Pamela Sue Fox__.

I give __903 Iceberg Road, Anchorage, Alaska__ to __James Eric Hanson__.

I give __Irish jewelry and my wedding ring__ to __Mary Natalie Swanson__.

I give __all jewelry not given above__ to __Kay Baxter and Mary Baxter__.

I give __$781.35__ to __Mary Natalie Swanson and Kevin Kilby__.

I give __Wells Fargo acct ending in #8923__ to __Lawrence Deer a hunting buddy__.

I give __all spare tires and auto parts__ to __Victor Perez my mechanic__.

I give _____ to _____.

3. SEPARATE WRITINGS. I may do writings separate from this Will to gift tangible personal property as allowed by state law, and all such writings should be followed. But any such writing not found within 90 days of my death is canceled and has no effect. A gift in such a writing to a person who does not survive me is canceled and has no effect. This Will does not revoke any such writings that now exist.

4. RESIDUE. I give the rest and residue and remainder of my estate, my money and property of any kind and nature, and anything I have an interest in so long as it was not transferred by other Will provisions (all of which is called the "residue"), as follows:

a) to _____Ruth May Baker_____ who survive me with persons just named who survive me taking the share of non-survivors, then if anything remains

b) to __45% to Oscar Elliot Baker,   and 45% to Karen Lisa Lundy, and 10% to Oscar Sanchez my friend_____ and if any of those just named do not survive me their part goes to their lineal descendants, per stirpes.

5. ADMINISTRATION. I name, nominate, and appoint __Ruth May Baker__ as Executor including for me, my Will, and my estate.

6. GUARDIAN. I name, nominate, and appoint _Amanda Sue Brubaker my sister_ to be if needed the Guardian of the Person of any minor child under age 18 of mine and to have care, authority, custody, and other control of them. I also name, nominate, and appoint this same person to be Guardian of the Estate over the property, money, and estate of any minor child and to have control, care, and power of these things.

7. MISCELLANEOUS. The following applies to this Will and generally.

In this Will no part left unfilled is a mistake including spaces in the residue clause.

The facts support and I want Ohio state law to apply to this Will and my estate.

I order that my just debts, funeral and related expenses, and taxes be paid as soon after my death as practical but only the items my Executor or Personal Representative chooses.

Priority of Will gifts of the same type is based on the order they are written.

If a gift or section in this Will reasonably mentions survival in any way then such survival is an absolute condition and anti-lapse laws or similar have no effect.

The words "give" and "gift" also means a devise, bequest, grant, legacy, or similar.

A gift of property no longer owned by me at death shall lapse and be of no effect including no payment of money shall be done in its place.

I am intentionally not providing by Will or other ways for some family, including I am not providing for some children of mine and also children of a deceased child of mine.

No earlier transfer reduces a Will gift unless I usually called it a loan or advancement.

Unless another meaning is shown use of plural includes the singular and vice versa, "they" can mean 1 person, and masculine, feminine, and neuter words are interchangeable.

Unless a Will specifically says otherwise a) a secured debt including a mortgage or lien shall not be paid off including by a Executor or similar or in probate, b) a recipient of a Will gift of property takes it subject to debts, and c) no recipient of property who later loses it or who pays to keep it may require others or the estate to pay or do exoneration.

I request and authorize any informal, summary, and quick probate or similar action. Any Executor or Personal Representative may act independently with no court supervision,

including independent administration, and with no inventory, appraisal, or other action.

I give any Executor or Personal Representative the a) fullest authority, discretion, and powers allowed by state law, b) power to lease, sell, mortgage, convey, or keep property including real property in a manner and time they deem helpful or proper, and c) authority to settle or pay claims or debts in the time and manner they in their sole discretion choose.

Any Executor or Personal Representative has sole discretion how to divide a gift to several persons, how to carry out a general gift, and how to do a gift to multiple persons.

Pay for any lawyer is what a Executor or Personal Representative agrees to and not a statutory fee or an amount suggested by a county or other local provision.

Any Guardian of any type, Conservator, Custodian, or other person managing a minor's property or money may use or invade the principal and sell property without court action.

The residue includes lapsed or failed gifts, insurance paid to the estate, digital assets, inheritances owed me, and all I had power of appointment or testamentary disposition over.

If evidence does not show it likely a person survived me by 120 hours (5 days) then for this Will and my estate they shall be deemed in all ways as having died before me.

If part of this Will is by law invalid or unenforceable other provisions remain in effect.

Any Executor or Personal Representative may at any time transfer money or property of a minor under age 18 to a Custodian to serve under the Ohio Uniform Transfers to Minors Act or a similar law anywhere, and may pick the person to be Custodian including they may pick themselves.

TESTATOR

IN WITNESS WHEREOF, I, _Paul Brian Baker_ sign, publish, and declare this instrument as my Will, this _30th_ day of _December_, 20_27_.

Paul Brian Baker
Testator signature

WITNESSES

The foregoing instrument was signed by the Testator and Testator declared it to be the Testator's Will, which signing and declaration was made in the presence of us the witnesses, and we do now sign our names in this document below as witnesses at the request and in the presence of the Testator and presence of each other on this the _30th_ day of _December_, 20_17_.

Olivia Joy Pawlenty 87 Hastings Avenue, Buffalo, OH 43987
Signature of Witness Address of Witness

Roy Felix Pawlenty 87 Hastings Avenue, Buffalo, OH 43987
Signature of Witness Address of Witness

**Sample Filled Out Form: Last Will and Testament (Standard)
with Will modified to have a 1 Part Residue Clause**

LAST WILL AND TESTAMENT

I, __John David Smith__, of __Lincoln County__, Ohio, do revoke all prior Wills and testamentary documents and do make, publish, and declare this as my Will. I am of sound mind and under no duress or undue influence and acting voluntarily.

1. LIST OF SPOUSE AND CHILDREN. To help show I am mentally competent and have sufficient memory to make a Will I wish to list any living spouse and living children I now have. I currently have the following living spouse and living children: __my son Adam Michael Smith__.

2. GIFTS. I give these gifts in this Will, but to get a gift in this section the recipient must survive me except as otherwise stated below.

I give __$200__ to __each of my nieces and nephews so about $2,800 in total__.

I give __$400__ to __Garner Food Shelf in Columbus, Ohio__.

I give __$300__ to __St. Joseph my old church in Aurora, Illinois__.

I give _____ to _____.

I give _____ to _____.

I give _____ to _____.

I give _____ to _____.

I give _____ to _____.

I give _____ to _____.

I give _____ to _____.

I give _____ to _____.

3. SEPARATE WRITINGS. I may do writings separate from this Will to gift tangible personal property as allowed by state law, and all such writings should be followed. But any such writing not found within 90 days of my death is canceled and has no effect. A gift in such a writing to a person who does not survive me is canceled and has no effect. This Will does not revoke any such writings that now exist.

4. RESIDUE. The rest and residue and remainder of my estate, my property of any kind and nature, and anything I have an interest in, I give to _Adam Michael Smith and Judy Paula Ford_ who survive me, and if any of those just named do not survive me their part goes to their lineal descendants per stirpes.

5. ADMINISTRATION. I nominate and appoint _Judy Paula Ford my sister_ as Personal Representative including for me, my Will, and my estate.

6. MISCELLANEOUS. The following applies to this Will and generally.

In this Will no part left unfilled is a mistake including spaces in the residue clause.

The facts support and I want Ohio state law to apply to this Will and my estate.

I order that my just debts, funeral and related expenses, and taxes be paid as soon after my death as practical but only the items my Executor or Personal Representative chooses.

Priority of Will gifts of the same type is based on the order they are written.

If a gift or section in this Will reasonably mentions survival in any way then such survival is an absolute condition and anti-lapse laws or similar have no effect.

The words "give" and "gift" also means a devise, bequest, grant, legacy, or similar.

A gift of property no longer owned by me at death shall lapse and be of no effect including no payment of money shall be done in its place.

Unless a Will gift specifies otherwise if a Will gift goes to multiple recipients if any do not survive me the part to them lapses and instead goes to other surviving recipients.

I am intentionally not providing by Will or other ways for some family, including I am not providing for some children of mine and also children of a deceased child of mine.

No earlier transfer reduces a Will gift unless I usually called it a loan or advancement.

Unless another meaning is shown use of plural includes the singular and vice versa, "they" can mean 1 person, and masculine, feminine, and neuter words are interchangeable.

Unless a Will specifically says otherwise a) a secured debt including a mortgage or lien shall not be paid off including by a Executor or similar or in probate, b) a recipient of a Will gift of property takes it subject to debts, and c) no recipient of property who later loses it or who pays to keep it may require others or the estate to pay or do exoneration.

I request and authorize any informal, summary, and quick probate or similar action. Any Executor or Personal Representative may act independently with no court supervision, including independent administration, and with no inventory, appraisal, or other action.

I give any Executor or Personal Representative the a) fullest authority, discretion, and powers allowed by state law, b) power to lease, sell, mortgage, convey, or keep property including real property in a manner and time they deem helpful or proper, and c) authority to settle or pay claims or debts in the time and manner they in their sole discretion choose.

Any Executor or Personal Representative has sole discretion how to divide a gift to several persons, how to carry out a general gift, and how to do a gift to multiple persons.

Pay for any lawyer is what a Executor or Personal Representative agrees to and not a statutory fee or an amount suggested by a county or other local provision.

Any Guardian of any type, Conservator, Custodian, or other person managing a minor's property or money may use or invade the principal and sell property without court action.

If context permits the terms Personal Representative and Executor and Administrator are interchangeable, Guardian of the Estate and Guardian of Property and Conservator and Custodian are interchangeable, and residue and residuary are interchangeable. Any such person may stand in place and act and have all powers like the others.

The residue includes lapsed or failed gifts, insurance paid to the estate, digital assets, inheritances owed me, and all I had power of appointment or testamentary disposition over.

Any Personal Representative, Executor, Administrator, Guardian of any type like for a person or estate, Conservator, Custodian, and any other fiduciary under this Will or otherwise shall qualify and serve without bond, surety, security, surety bond, or similar.

If evidence does not show it likely a person survived me by 120 hours (5 days) then for this Will and my estate they shall be deemed in all ways as having died before me.

If part of this Will is by law invalid or unenforceable other provisions remain in effect.

Any Executor or Personal Representative may at any time transfer money or property of a minor under age 18 to a Custodian to serve under the Ohio Uniform Transfers to Minors Act or a similar law anywhere, and may pick the person to be Custodian including they may pick themselves.

TESTATOR

IN WITNESS WHEREOF, I, _John David Smith_ did sign, publish, and declare this instrument as my Will, this _22nd_ day of _July_, 20_21_.

John David Smith
Signature of Testator

WITNESSES

The foregoing instrument was signed by the Testator and Testator declared it to be the Testator's Will, which signing and declaration was made in the presence of us the witnesses, and we do now sign our names in this document below as witnesses at the request and in the presence of the Testator and presence of each other on this _22nd_ day of _July_, 20_21_.

Susan Harriet Rogers   _87 Badger Road, Chatham, OH 44913_
Signature of Witness   Address of Witness

Lucy Ann Pamway   _892 Franklin Street, Ohio, NY 10887_
Signature of Witness   Address of Witness